Advanced Praise

"*Anxiety Unpacked* feels like sitting down with a wise, grounded friend who gently says, "Let's make sense of this together." Noelle McWard Aquino brings decades of clinical experience — and deep personal insight as a mother — to guide readers through the tangled roots of anxiety with warmth, clarity, and compassion. She dismantles the myth that anxiety is a one-size-fits-all struggle. This isn't just another book on anxiety — it's *the roadmap anxious people have been looking for*. Aquino introduces a simple yet profound model that categorizes anxiety into three root causes — catastrophizing, control, and distorted beliefs — and gives you the exact tools to target each one. Whether you've tried everything or you're just beginning to understand your anxiety, this book offers something rare: real hope. Packed with actionable strategies, moving case studies, and personal stories that make you feel seen, *Anxiety Unpacked* doesn't just offer relief — it offers transformation.

If you've ever thought, "Why hasn't anyone explained it to me this way before?" — this book is your answer."

Matthias Barker, Psychotherapist and Founder of Estrangement.com

In *Anxiety Unpacked*, Noelle McWard Aquino offers an empathetic trail map through the wild world of anxiety. Drawing wisdom from neurobiology, human development, and the complexities of mothering an anxious child, Noelle sensitively explores why anxiety is not a one-size-fits-all experience. With deep compassion and genuine care, she encourages readers to befriend their anxious parts rather than push them away. Her deep clinical wisdom shines through as she equips you with practical strategies that are easily woven throughout daily life. Many heartfelt case examples reflect your own struggles, demonstrating that you are not alone in this journey. *Anxiety Unpacked* serves as a nurturing companion; helping you navigate your anxious thoughts and feelings with kindness and understanding, guiding you back toward the fulfilling and meaningful life that you truly deserve. If you, like myself, are a person for whom anxiety has been a lifelong companion, you will find this book to be a treasure trove of accessible tools to gently support anxious parts in finding their way through a world full of significant challenge and beauty.

Lara Krawchuk, MSW, LCSW, MPH
Grief expert, IFS consultant and owner of Healing Perspectives (www.yourhealingperspectives.com)

"As a therapist who works with survivors of relational trauma, I find that many of my clients struggle with daily anxiety that, as Noelle puts it: 'fights to remain in control when challenged'. As someone who lives with anxiety, I understand all too well how difficult it can feel to shake off! Thank you, Noelle, for addressing this issue and for supporting those who live with anxiety every day!"

Kaytee Gillis, LCSW, Psychotherapist and author of four books, including *Breaking the Cycle: the 6 Stages of Healing from Childhood Family Trauma; and Healing from Parental Abandonment and Neglect.*

Noelle McWard Aquino has written a book for all of us over-functioners who are gripped by anxiety. In *Anxiety Unpacked*, McWard Aquino demystifies anxiety by offering explanations and solutions, all of which are grounded in the body. This book offers hope, comfort, and practical exercises for anyone who is attempting-- and failing-- to control their world only to find themselves more and more anxious and miserable.

Christie Tate
NYT bestseller Author
GROUP: How One Therapist and a Circle of Strangers Saved My Life
B.F.F.: A Memoir of Friendship Lost & Found

In Anxiety Unpacked, Noelle has skillfully provided readers with a route to interrupt the patterns that could otherwise disrupt our lives with unchecked thoughts and beliefs about the world and ourselves. Having the tools to unravel and challenge the faulty narratives that we create can help anyone feeling stuck in ongoing anxiety. What a gift to have Noelle's years of successful clinical work be presented in such an approachable and immediately applicable way.

Courtney Rolfe, LCPC, ModernMindandHeart.com and co-author of *Polyvagal Prompts: Finding Connection and Joy Through Guided Explorations* by Deb Dana and Courtney Rolfe

"*Anxiety Unpacked* perfectly balances compelling, relatable stories and practical, professional guidance for anyone struggling with anxiety. The way the author presents three distinct anxiety types puts a fresh spin on information I thought I knew. I've lived with anxiety for most of my life and have read a lot on the topic, but this book helped me see it, and myself, in a new way. Now, thanks to this guide, I have a new level of understanding---and a more complete toolbox for navigating challenges. If you're looking for fresh insights and a clearer path forward, this book is a must-read."

Tammy Letherer, award winning author of *The Buddha At My Table: How I found Peace in Betrayal and Divorce.*

anxiety unpacked

Discover Your Type and Recover Your Peace

Noelle McWard Aquino

Printed in the United States of America

Hardcover ISBN: 978-1-960876-89-8

Paperback ISBN: 978-1-960876-90-4

Library of Congress Control Number: 2025934780

Dedication

This book is dedicated to my clients and my son - who have taught me more about anxiety and what it means to persevere and flourish in life with it – than any theory of psychology ever has.

Access Bonus Content in the Book Portal

Enjoy exclusive bonus material designed to complement your reading experience!

Scan the QR code below with your mobile device to access worksheets, exclusive videos, resources, and playlists to complement your experience with this book and further support your healing journey.

No sign-up required — just scan and enjoy!

Having trouble with the QR code?

Visit: https://noellemcwardaquino.com/anxiety-unpacked

Table of Contents

I Worried

By Mary Oliver

I worried a lot. Will the garden grow, will the rivers

flow in the right direction,

will the earth turn as it was taught, and if not how shall

I correct it?

Was I right, was I wrong, will I be forgiven,

can I do better?

Will I ever be able to sing, even the sparrows

can do it and I am, well,

hopeless.

Is my eyesight fading or am I just imagining it,

am I going to get rheumatism,

lockjaw, dementia?

Finally, I saw that worrying came to nothing.

And gave it up. And took my old body

and went out into the morning and sang.

Noelle McWard Aquino

Introduction

Why Another Book About Anxiety?

I went to sleep early that night. My phone was set to silent, as it always is at bedtime. My teenage son was staying at his father's house. When I woke up in the morning, there were 64 texts and 21 missed calls from my son. The text messages read like this:

Mom
Mom
Mom
Mom
Are you there?
Mom
Mom
Mom
Mom

Over and over. Sixty-four times.

The missed calls had come in one right after the other.

The last call was followed by a text message saying, "I am really anxious, and I am walking back to the house."

I found him asleep in his bed, having walked the mile distance from his dad's house to mine in the middle of a cold December night. I felt both relieved to see him safe and peacefully sleeping and sick that I had not woken up in his efforts to reach me.

This is a scene from my front row view of my son's anxiety.

When I began my career as a psychotherapist in 1993, I was strongly drawn to working with clients struggling with anxiety disorders. I often wondered why since I do not suffer from anxiety, beyond being a human being. Yet, I was compelled by the urgency and distress often present in my anxious clients. It was this same urgency that led to my feelings of inadequacy early in my career when working with the tools I had acquired up to that point. I felt ill prepared to sufficiently help my anxious clients find relief from their suffering and distress.

Wishing to do more to support my clients, I pursued additional training to enhance my skills in treating anxiety disorders. I studied many of the available evidence-based theories and models that have been proven to remedy it. All were helpful, offering wisdom and value. Yet what I discovered was that no one thing was THE thing. No one approach offered the solution to the many facets of anxiety. Anxiety is not a "one size fits all" problem. It is a term that is used quite broadly to describe an experience that is varied and nuanced.

I now had many possible solutions and sought to figure out which ones would best help with which manifestations of anxiety. It was a puzzle I wished to solve, and the answers I arrived at helped form the Anxiety Unpacked model. While the genesis for creating the Anxiety Unpacked model was professional, I did not realize at the time how relevant it would become for me personally as I would later become the mother of an anxious child.

From the time he was young, it was evident to our family and his teachers that my son grappled with an anxiety disorder. The effects of anxiety have been varied and persistent, impacting many aspects of his life. As his mother, I have witnessed first-hand his distress and many challenges.

Whether it was the near-daily meltdowns over his fear of not finishing homework - no matter how little he had or how much time was available to do it - or his distress in third grade when his teacher announced it was time to move on to a new activity before he'd completed his work, the pattern was clear. No amount of reassurance could quiet his fear that leaving something unfinished would lead to something bad. He struggled to adjust when plans were disrupted, or schedules changed. He avoided activities he once loved, convinced he had done something wrong and that others would be upset with him. The examples could go on and on.

What began as a professional interest in improving my ability to treat anxiety took on new meaning as I helped my son navigate his own.

Beyond the many approaches I studied, my way of thinking about and working with anxiety is informed by patterns I consistently noticed among my clients. Regardless of the details of their anxiety or the variations in their backgrounds and histories, I observed recurring themes in how they described their anxiety and how it fought to preserve itself.

What took shape was the conceptualization that all my clients' unique and varied experiences with anxiety could be categorized as stemming from one of three main sources. Though the details were always different, the characteristics of each source of anxiety were the same and always present. This then informed how I intervened, targeting the interventions to the traits and needs represented by each root cause of anxiety.

The three root causes are:

- Catastrophizing
- Control
- Distorted beliefs

As I worked with clients from this framework, I observed they were making greater improvements around their anxiety and more quickly. This encouraged me to begin explaining the root causes to my clients, and the solutions required by each. And something noteworthy and important began to happen. Consistently—and without exception—every single client was immediately able to identify the root of their anxiety. They would say things like, "I experience one but not the other two," "I deal with two but not the third," or "I relate to all three."

Over the years, I have had numerous clients – many of whom have had previous therapy for their chronic anxiety – say to me, "Why has no one ever told me this before?" "I never thought about it that way before, but that makes sense," "You have helped me more with my anxiety than any other therapist I have worked with," or "I have made more progress with you than I have with any previous therapy." I believe the reason for this feedback is that I was offering something different than what had been provided in earlier therapies.

A pivotal moment for me was when Sue, a previous client whom I had counseled before the development of this model, re- engaged in therapy with me.

Sue was a young, successful, well put together, and kind professional woman who was highly stressed and exhibited rigid behavior and high expectations of herself and others. In our earlier work together, these behaviors had seemed intractable, and I eventually attributed them to her personality.

Upon Sue's return to therapy following the development of the Anxiety Unpacked model, I quickly realized that the traits were, in fact, deeply intertwined with anxiety rooted in a need for control. Armed with this new understanding and the Anxiety Unpacked model, I had a clear roadmap for addressing these concerns.

Our therapy sessions focused on freeing Sue from her behavioral patterns by delving into her need for control. We implemented strategies and interventions designed to specifically release the need for control and to develop more flexible and adaptive behaviors.

One day, Sue came into therapy and said, for the first time ever, "I'm really happy. I'm not stressed like I used to be. I feel like I'm living my best life." She then went on to identify numerous ways in which her behavior had dramatically changed and in ways that now felt effortless. Sue's only concern was her ability to maintain these changes. However, she came in week after week, reporting that she continued to feel happy and relaxed and that the changes were unfolding naturally, with little effort on her part.

In one of our final sessions, Sue said to me, "I feel like a different person now. I never would have believed it was possible for me to feel this way. I felt like I kept talking you into circles, but you kept telling me this was possible. Thank you for sticking with me to get me here." I could see that Sue was lighter and more relaxed, and I felt elated for her.

Just as anxiety presents in many different ways, recovery can also take many different forms. Yet I consistently see profound changes when those suffering from anxiety are provided with an understanding of their anxiety that makes sense, an awareness of how their anxiety fights to remain in control when challenged, and the tools and practices that best address the root cause. This is what the Anxiety Unpacked Model offers.

After experiencing the success of the Anxiety Unpacked model with my clients, I began training therapists in the hope that it, too, would help them and their clients. Therapists who trained with me signed up for consultation groups or individual supervision, all of which affirmed to me that the model was offering something new and valuable to their work.

My hope in writing this book is that it will help you - whether you are someone who suffers from anxiety or a professional who treats it - to better understand anxiety and feel more empowered in your ability to manage or treat it. Perhaps you, too, will read something in the pages that follow and think, "I never thought about it that way before but that makes sense!" And with this new understanding and the tools provided, you will gain newfound confidence in your ability to address your anxiety in a meaningful way.

Beyond the many clients I have had the honor to work with, I have witnessed through my son the pain and challenges of acute and chronic anxiety that often feels overpowering. I have great empathy and admiration for those who navigate life with its added burden and weight. My wish is that this book will bring relief through a deeper understanding of your anxiety and what you can do about it.

So, let's begin.

Chapter 1

**Anxiety: Why We're
Wired To Feel It.**

Several years ago, I was invited to guest lecture at a
law school to teach about trauma to a class
preparing to conduct political asylum interviews. I had
taught in graduate school settings before, and while I
enjoy teaching, my nervous system does not like
speaking in front of a crowd. I have always been shy
and do not like being the center of attention, all eyes on
me.

Before the class began, though I was comfortable
with the material, I had "butterflies" in my stomach and
felt a bit nauseous. As I began teaching, I felt a little
warm and flushed, and my heart started beating very
fast, so fast that my breath became shallower and
shallower. I began to sound out of breath until finally, I
could not speak at all.

What was happening, and why did my body react in
this way? It was doing what it was designed to do in
the face of perceived danger.

As humans, we are wired with biological functions and responses that are rooted in our evolutionary drive to survive. Anxiety is tied to the autonomic nervous system, which is responsible for regulating emotion and responding to threats and danger.

The autonomic nervous system is controlled by the amygdala, a cluster of cells located near the base of your brain. It is one of the most primitive parts of the human brain and performs a function shared by all living organisms. The amygdala's only job is to look for signs of threat or danger and then trigger the body to respond when danger is detected to enable your survival.

When the amygdala perceives a threat, it triggers the release of hormones, cortisol and adrenaline amongst them. These hormones activate the sympathetic nervous system, whose only purpose is to fend off danger and ensure survival, preparing the body to fight or flee. This sympathetic nervous system response is commonly known as the "fight, flight, or freeze response".

Adrenaline causes a number of physiological responses. It increases your blood pressure and heart rate, improves blood flow to muscles and organs, and elevates your breathing rate. Other responses include dilated pupils, widened eyelids (deer in headlights), stimulated sweat glands, dilated blood vessels in the large muscles, constricted blood vessels in the rest of the body, and an inhibition of secretions into the digestive system, conserving energy that otherwise would be used for digestion.

All of these functions serve to fuel the parts of your body that are essential to your survival while conserving energy that would otherwise be directed to non-essential functions. Additionally, when the sympathetic nervous system is triggered, unneeded parts of the prefrontal cortex (the highest-level thinking part of the brain) go off-line so that your brain power can be focused only on the danger and the cognitive functions needed to survive.

You may recognize your symptoms of anxiety (and mine that I described at the beginning of this chapter) through this list of physiological responses to adrenaline. The increased heart rate often accompanying anxiety, aids in more blood and oxygen quickly reaching the muscles and extremities, powering them to either fight the source of danger or flee from it. This would come in handy if you were encountering real danger, giving you the strength needed to fight off or run away from the threat. But, when you're standing in front of a classroom, it can be paralyzing (and embarrassing). Likewise, the shallow breathing (or hyperventilation) that many experience is due to an elevated respiratory response, whose purpose is to send more oxygen to the muscles. Becoming flushed and shaking are the result of excess blood and energy that are created but don't get used.

Sweating is the result of stimulated sweat glands, intended to cool the body in its activated state. Feeling nauseous is due to the slowing of your digestive system to divert energy from functions unnecessary for your immediate survival. The heightened focus on problems and danger that accompanies anxiety exists because the brain automatically hyper-focuses on the perceived danger to better attend to it.

Lastly, because some of your prefrontal cortex functions temporarily go off-line to engage only those needed to attend to the danger, you lose access to your more rational thought processes. This contributes to difficulty controlling your thoughts and feelings of excess worry.

In his 1995 book *"Emotional Intelligence: Why it Can Matter More Than IQ,"* psychologist Daniel Goleman named this overreaction to stress or perceived threat "amygdala hijack." In amygdala hijack, the fight or flight response overrides and disables the rational, reasoned responses of the prefrontal cortex. In other words, if you become "irrational" when anxious, it is not a personal flaw or failure and it is not your fault. You have literally lost access to parts of your brain that allow for more rational thinking. Yet, there are things you can do to bring you back to these lost functions. We will talk about them soon.

This highly sophisticated survival mechanism contains one significant flaw: it cannot differentiate between a threat and danger that is real, and one that is perceived. If your mind perceives danger, your body will react exactly as it was designed to do. Those who suffer from chronic and persistent anxiety have habitual and often unconscious ways of perceiving danger that is not there. These habitual and unconscious patterns form the three root causes of anxiety.

Noelle McWard Aquino

Chapter 2

The Five Universal
Truths of Anxiety

In introducing the concept of the three root causes of anxiety, I wish to differentiate between recognizable manifestations of anxiety (the three root causes), and the unique source of your anxiety. Many factors can influence the presence of anxiety, including your neurobiology, personality traits, temperament, family of origin dynamics, life experiences, societal and cultural factors, and trauma history.

Regardless of the source or presentation of your anxiety and before delving into the three root causes and their unique solutions, let's first explore the five universal truths of anxiety. These are facts of anxiety that are always present, no matter the root cause. Understanding them is essential to your journey of overcoming anxiety.

Truth One: Breathing is Essential

It has been my experience that while many with anxiety have been told to breathe when feeling anxious, far fewer have been told why or how to breathe. I want you to understand both.

Recalling the sympathetic nervous system response that occurs when the amygdala is activated, anxiety is a physiologically aroused state. There is adrenaline coursing through your system, energizing your body to fight or flee. The more heightened this state of arousal, the more intense the anxiety – ranging from mild to a full-blown panic attack.

When done properly, deep breathing is the fastest and most effective way to calm this physiological arousal. From a biological and physiological standpoint, you cannot do deep breathing and remain in a physiologically aroused state at the same time. Thus, breathing is not only a highly effective tool to utilize when anxious, but also an essential one.

Deep breathing and relaxation techniques activate the parasympathetic nervous system, which sends a signal to your brain that you are safe and don't need to engage the fight, flight, or freeze response. It is what helps the body to relax and returns it to a natural state after periods of stress or danger. Deep breathing also gets more oxygen to the thinking brain, giving you more access to the rational and meaning-making functions of your prefrontal cortex.

There are many different breathing techniques you can employ when anxious, each are effective. What most share in common is a slower exhale than inhale. It is the slow, prolonged exhale that calms physiological arousal. The goal is to slow your exhalation to the greatest extent possible to bring your body back to a state of equilibrium and calm.

A second important trait of effective breathing is to breathe from the diaphragm. To check if you're engaging in diaphragmatic breathing, place your hand on your stomach. As you inhale, you should feel your stomach gently rise, pushing against your hand, like a balloon filling with air. When you exhale, your stomach should gently fall as the air slowly releases. This deep, controlled breathing activates your body's natural relaxation response.

Here are some breathing techniques for you to try. All will work. You can practice each and use whichever feels most comfortable and practical for you.

The 4-7-8 Breathing Method:

The 4-7-8 breathing method was developed by Dr. Andrew Weil, who describes it as a "natural tranquilizer for the system." To prepare yourself to use the 4-7-8 breathing method, first do some practice breaths with your hand on your stomach to ensure that your breath is originating from your diaphragm. Inhale through your nostrils, and exhale through pursed lips, making a "whoosh" sound as you exhale.

19

Next, inhale for the count of four, hold your breath for the count of seven, and then slowly exhale for the count of eight. You may find it difficult to exhale to the full count of eight. If so, keep your focus on exhaling as slowly as possible, increasing the exhale count with each round until you can exhale to the full count of eight. Repeat this cycle of breathing until your body has returned to a state of calm. If you do not get immediate relief, stick with it. Eventually, it will calm your nervous system and help you feel more regulated.

Hand on Heart and Belly Technique:

Place one hand on your heart and one hand on your belly. It may feel natural to close your eyes as you do this. Inhale, starting in your diaphragm and moving all the way up to the top of your lungs, and then slowly exhale. Continue breathing slowly, in and out, as you keep your hand on your heart and belly. In addition to the relaxation brought on by diaphragmatic breathing, placing your hand on your heart is experienced by your body as being held and supported.

Box Breathing:

In this method, you will create a "box" with your breath by inhaling for the count of four, holding your breath for the count of four, exhaling to the count of four, and then holding your breath for the count of four. Repeat this pattern of breathing for as long as is needed to return your body to a state of relaxation and calm.

Alternating Nostril Breathing:

This is a breathing method that comes from yogic practice. As such, both the inhale and exhale will be through your nose. To begin, place both feet on the ground and sit with a straight, upward posture (not slumped or slouching). With your right hand, close your right nostril with your thumb. Inhale fully through your left nostril. Next, close your left nostril with the index finger of your right hand while releasing your thumb over your right nostril and exhale through your right nostril. Keep your left nostril closed with your index finger, and inhale through your right nostril. Close your right nostril with your right thumb while releasing your index finger over your left nostril and exhale through the left nostril. This is one full breath cycle. Repeat this pattern for up to five minutes.

Truth Two: The Most Common Response to Anxiety is Avoidance

When feeling anxious, the most common human response is to avoid the source of your anxiety. While avoidance may provide a temporary feeling of relief, in the long run, it only magnifies anxiety. Avoidance is always prolonged suffering disguised as safety. The more you avoid something, the more power gets attached to it, amplifying your feelings of stress or anxiety. At best, avoidance heightens your anxiety, and at worst, it turns a perceived outcome into an actualized problem.

An inescapable truth is the only way to overcome anxiety is to step into it. It is not possible to overcome anxiety from a distance or by thinking yourself out of it. Avoidance will never deliver relief, and it keeps you a prisoner of your fears.

Lisa, a small business owner, experienced anxiety when receiving emails from clients making requests she knew she was going to decline. Her fear was that by saying no, the client would become angry and write a negative Yelp review, future clients would choose not to work with her because of the bad review, and her business would be ruined. Consequently, Lisa delayed responding to client emails to avoid delivering a negative response and the perceived catastrophic consequences. All the while, the unanswered emails sat in her inbox, awaiting a response, which magnified and prolonged her anxiety. The longer she took to respond, the greater the likelihood the client would in fact be upset, not necessarily by the response itself, but by the lateness of her response.

I worked with Lisa on facing her fear by responding right away to the requests. Doing so accomplished several things: it allowed her to test the validity of her fears (none were accurate), and it shortened the duration and intensity of her anxiety. By repeated practice, Lisa found that her fear attached to saying no diminished in direct proportion to how quickly she stepped *into* the anxiety.

There are many forms of avoidance, and avoidant behavior often becomes symptomatic behavior. Avoidance of emotional pain is commonly sought through the use of substances, food, sex, shopping, and cutting/self-harm, to name a few. These avoidant behaviors can become disordered when the need to avoid feelings is persistent and chronic. Symptoms of anxiety such as over-analyzing, rumination, and keeping yourself overly busy can also be attempts to avoid uncomfortable emotions, trading one discomfort for another that is more tolerable to you.

Developing awareness of your avoidant behaviors will be a necessary step in your journey of overcoming anxiety.

Truth Three: The Mind Can Hold Only One Thought at a Time

While your mind can easily (and sometimes quickly) jump from one thought to another, it can hold only one thought at a time. If your mind is focused on an anxiety-producing thought, anxiety will follow. Conversely, if your mind is focused on non-anxious or calming thoughts, you will experience ease and calm. Imagine studying for an exam, and the difference between going into it thinking, "This test will be too hard, and I am going to fail!" versus, "I have studied and prepared, and I can do this."

Part of the physiology of anxiety is that your brain hyper-focuses on perceived danger to marshal all your

internal resources for survival. This can create a
heightened focus on worry or fearful thoughts and
accompanying feelings of anxiety. However, when you
consciously redirect your attention to either a neutral or
calming thought – such as a soothing mantra, imagining
a peaceful place, or recalling a positive memory – you
activate the parasympathetic nervous system. This
counteracts the stress response, interrupting the anxiety
loop and easing the return to a more balanced and
relaxed state.

Consciously redirecting your thoughts can be a
powerful coping strategy when dealing with anxiety.
Ultimately, the goal is to feel all your emotions without
being overwhelmed by them. And while feeling your
feelings is necessary, there is no inherent value in sitting
in feelings that overwhelm you. Rather, you must build
your capacity to fully experience your emotions.
Coping strategies that increase your tolerance for your
feelings help strengthen that capacity.

There are many ways to use intentional distraction
as a tool for managing the symptoms of anxiety. You
may try repeating a mantra that is soothing and
calming. Examples of this may be:

I am safe.

All is well.

I can do this.

I can handle this.

I can be uncomfortable and safe at the same time.

Listening to music and singing out loud to further engage your brain is an effective way of disrupting anxiety by engaging your brain in something pleasurable.

Using a meditation app is another effective tool. They offer guided practices, making the use of meditation more accessible, especially for beginners. Apps offer a variety of styles of meditation, as well as specific focuses of content such as anxiety relief, sleep improvement, increased ability to focus, and stress management.

One day, my son and I were gathering our coats, about to leave the house to go to his play rehearsal, when he had a panic attack. He was completely overcome, crying, hyperventilating and insisting that he could not go to rehearsal. I tried to reassure him and guide him in taking deep breaths with me, but in his heightened and dysregulated state, he insisted he was unable to.

I noticed his script sitting on the table next to us. I opened it and began to read out loud from the script, asking him to join me. At first, he resisted. But I kept reading aloud, encouraging him to join me. Eventually, he did. Within less than a minute of reading aloud, he began to calm and regulate. After a few more short moments of reading, he had returned to a state of enough calm and self-regulation that we were able to leave the house and go to his rehearsal.

The act of reading out loud from his script had shifted his brain's focus from his anxious thoughts to something neutral, thereby interrupting his intense anxiety response and allowing him to become regulated. Thus, he was able to go to rehearsal, stepping into rather than avoiding the perceived danger, further disrupting his anxiety.

To be clear, avoidance and distraction are not the same thing. Avoidance is an action to bypass the source of your anxiety. Distraction is a tool you can use when engaging with the source of your anxiety to help you tolerate the discomfort you feel. It provides a way to step into anxiety and not feel overwhelmed by it. If you are afraid of flying, avoidance would be to never fly. Distraction would be to board an airplane and use tools such as meditation, listening to soothing music, or favorite podcasts to lessen your discomfort while flying.

I have always been acutely afraid of heights. An intense visceral anxiety accompanies this fear. During my high school years, there were two amusement parks close to my house, which I visited with friends. Due to my intense fear of heights, I hated roller coasters – everything about them. So, naturally, I avoided them. However, wanting to join my friends, who all loved roller coasters, I forced myself to ride them.

As the car made its slow ascent up the big hills, I would take long, slow, deep breaths and repeat silently to myself, "I am okay. I am okay. I am okay". This was effective enough that I could tolerate the anguishing slow ascent up and the hurling descent down the hills.

Eventually, I started to enjoy the roller coasters and was able to ride even the most challenging ones. Unknowingly, I was practicing some of the key skills that are essential to managing anxiety: exposure (stepping into the anxiety), deep breathing, and placing my attention on a non-anxiety producing thought (mantras).

Truth Four: When in Emotionally Charged Situations, Your Mind Will Create a Story Representing Your Greatest Fear and Vulnerability. The Story Will Rarely Be True.

As humans, we are uncomfortable with uncertainty. Our minds respond to this discomfort by automatically and often unconsciously creating stories in an attempt to make known the unknown. In all situations, there will be things you know:

- What you can observe
- What someone directly tells you about what they are thinking or feeling
- Common knowledge or known facts about the circumstance

And there will be things you don't know:

- Why someone is behaving in a way that you observe
- What someone else is thinking
- What someone else is feeling

When in an emotionally charged situation (anything that is important to you or has meaning for you), your mind will make up a story to fill in the blanks around what you don't know. The story will always be a representation of your greatest fear or vulnerability. And the story will rarely, if ever, be true.

This will show up in the form of statements such as, "I am sure his intention was X", "I know she was thinking this when she did that", "Of course he did it on purpose!", "I think her plan all along was to get me to do X", "She must be thinking X about me", and so on when describing events and circumstances in your life.

In moments of distress, if you step back and separate the facts you know from the story you are telling yourself, you will likely find the source of your distress is much more about the story than the facts. I wish I had a mathematical formula that proved the accuracy of these stories is statistically insignificant. I have none. But if you consider the likelihood that someone else's actions are motivated by the exact thing that is your greatest fear and vulnerability, or that they are thinking/feeling the exact thing that would be your greatest pain point, you may recognize why your story rarely reflects reality. This is perhaps one of the most overlooked facts of anxiety. The human propensity towards creating stories to fill in the blank space of the unknown or unknowable is pervasive and often harmful.

Because this response is universal, I know of no way to prevent it from happening. However, by understanding this human response in moments of emotional distress, you can separate out the facts, disengage from the story, and attend to only what you know to be true. It is also important to be aware of the behavior you engage in because you believe the story to be true and look for opportunities to align your behaviors or reactions to the facts rather than the story you have created.

I was acutely aware of these internal dynamics many years ago on a service trip to Malawi with my then teenage daughter. We were there to help build a school in a rural village, working side by side with the villagers. One day, the local women broke into joyous song and dance on the worksite. Everyone stopped working to cheer on the spontaneous celebration. Several of the American women jumped in, trying to replicate the dance, to the immense delight of the local women.

By nature, I am shy and reserved. I instinctively felt inhibited and too self-conscious to join the dancing. These are the facts of what was happening. I was also aware of a story attached to this experience – that I was invisible and that my presence held no value to those assembled because I was not joining in the dancing. *I* had no value. I experienced an immediate and intense feeling of shame.

This was not an unfamiliar feeling nor an unfamiliar story. It is one that I knew had deep roots, tracing all the way back to early childhood. The feeling associated with this story was powerful, and I had a familiar go-to response for this feeling; either leave the situation or avoid it. But here I was in a rural village in an African country with no place to go. So, I was forced to deal with it.

Fortunately, I was aware of what was happening. I understood that the belief I was invisible and of no value was a story I was imposing on the situation. Knowing this did not make the feelings go away, but it helped me to disengage from the story and focus instead on the facts, and to choose a response that aligned with the facts rather than my story.

I took a few moments to silently talk myself through this and then focused on enjoying and cheering on the local women and Americans who were joyfully celebrating. I did this while still feeling uncomfortable. By redirecting my conscious thoughts and attention and choosing a response that lined up with the facts rather than my story, the feelings subsided. Had I been in a different setting where I could have chosen my go-to response (to leave), I likely would have continued to be attached to the story I had automatically imposed on the situation, leaving it unchallenged.

Truth Five: There Is an Ever-Present Interplay Between Thoughts, Feelings and Behavior. Feelings are Always the Last to Change.

At all times, there is an interplay between your thoughts, feelings (emotional and visceral) and behavior in which one influences the others. A thought can create a feeling, both of which can influence behavior. A feeling may lead to thoughts and accompanying behavior. One never exists in the absence of the others.

For example, you might be invited to a social event where you don't know anyone attending and think, "People will notice that I'm alone and see me as strange. I'll feel uncomfortable talking to people I don't know." This thought will likely lead to feelings of anxiety around attending the event. These feelings of anxiety may influence your behavior in any number of ways: trying on multiple outfits as you search for the "right outfit" so that you will fit in, waiting for others to approach you at the event rather than seeking out others, or perhaps avoiding the event altogether.

Or you may wake up one day feeling anxious, noticing a knot in your stomach and a feeling of unease, and seek to find an explanation for this feeling. This may take the form of replaying a conversation from the previous day and deciding, without any objective confirmation, that something you said offended the person you were speaking with, and now they are mad at you. Having latched onto a thought that provides an

31

explanation for your feelings, not only will your feeling of anxiety be reinforced, but you may now feel compelled to either avoid that individual or reach out to them with an (unnecessary) apology.

Because one influences the others, this also means that intervening with one changes the others. If, in the first example, you were to change your thought about the social event from "I will feel uncomfortable talking to people I don't know" to "This will be a nice opportunity to meet new people", the feelings attached to the event may change, as might your behavior.

Likewise, if you wake up in the morning, feeling anxious and think to yourself, "I'm noticing that I am feeling anxiety in my stomach, let me take a few minutes to breathe and settle myself before I start my day", the feeling will likely shift. This change will be the result of choosing a behavior that seeks to attend to your feelings rather than reacting to them.

However, it is important to know that feelings are always the last thing to change. This truth in part explains why overcoming anxiety can be so challenging. Even if you logically and rationally know something is not true, if you feel that it is, you will act as if it is. Between thoughts and feelings, feelings are always the more powerful influencers.

Often, your first impulse will be to wait for the feeling to change before changing your thoughts or behavior. It is often hard to do or think something different while still feeling the same uncomfortable feelings.

The bad news is there is no way to change the feeling first. When has it ever helped to be told, "Just don't feel that way," or "How about you feel this instead?" Feelings don't work that way; they arise spontaneously and are beyond your control. You feel what you feel. However, the good news is that you can change your thoughts and actions, even when you feel uncomfortable or afraid. And when you do, the feelings will follow. By thinking, acting and choosing in accordance with your values, who you want to be, and how you want to show up in the world and then noticing the result of doing so, your feelings will change.

Knowing this is important for two reasons. First to set your expectations and second so you can practice the calming techniques recommended earlier in this chapter to help you manage and tolerate the discomfort of doing something new and unfamiliar. Your feelings will be the last thing to change; practicing breathing, meditation, and distraction will lessen the discomfort, and stepping into the anxiety rather than avoiding it is necessary to overcome it.

Chapter 3

The Mind-Body Connection

The mind and the body are interconnected, despite often being treated as separate entities. The brain is part of the body, not separate from it, and there is a two-way communication system between them. The state of one significantly influences the other. If your body is in pain, experiencing illness, or overly sedentary, your mental health and sense of well-being can be impacted. If your thoughts are fearful, stressed, depressed, etc., your physical body and health may be affected. Just as your brain communicates with the body, directing its actions and states of being, the body communicates with the brain, altering its perception of safety, connection, and well-being.

What this means is that anxiety that shows up in your body (as it always does) must be attended to within the body. You cannot only use your mind to address anxiety that is manifesting in physical symptoms and sensations. You must intervene directly with your body. And, when you attend to your body, it will affect the way your brain interprets your state of safety, making anxiety relief more accessible.

Learning to pay attention to your body and how emotions are expressed through it is a necessary part of the process of emotion regulation. Incorporating practices that are body centered will enhance your ability to effectively navigate anxiety. Here are some practices to use in conjunction with the tools and strategies contained within this book to help you become more attuned to your body and how to attend to it.

Recognizing where and how you feel anxiety in your body:

Tuning into your body, at any given moment, to notice what is felt and where is an essential skill to practice. If you stop what you are doing right now, and turn your attention inward, what sensations do you notice? Do you feel discomfort anywhere? Where in your body do you feel it, and what does it feel like?

Anxiety is always accompanied by physical manifestations. Many of these were discussed in Chapter 1 when describing the physiological arousal caused by the presence of adrenaline in your bloodstream. However, there are additional ways in which you may feel and hold anxiety in your body. These include:

- Muscle tension or tightness (think shoulders, jaw, and hands/clenched fists)

- Tightness in the stomach, chest and throat.
- Pins and needles sensations or numbness in your hands and/or feet.
- Brain fog or headaches.

Noticing the physical sensations of anxiety in your body at any given moment provides you with valuable information and important guidance on how to take care of your body as it relates to anxiety. Always remember that if you are in a heightened state of anxiety, your rational brain will not be available to you until the activation in your body is attended to.

Progressive Muscle Relaxation:

Once you have identified physical tension and tightness in your body, progressive muscle relaxation is an effective practice to relieve muscle tension. By releasing the tension being held in your muscles, your body will feel more relaxed, which will, in turn, cue your brain that you are safe.

There are three ways to approach progressive muscle relaxation – all are effective. The first is to tighten all your muscles, contracting them as a whole, and then releasing them all at once, making your body as loose and like a "wet noodle" as possible. Another approach is to tighten one muscle group at a time and then release them. Lastly, you can lie in a relaxed position (for example, Shavasana from yoga) and focus your attention on one muscle group at a time, starting either at the top of your head or your feet, and working your way through the body. As you focus on each muscle group or part of the body, notice any tightness that is present, and on bringing relaxation to whatever tension you find.

As I have practiced paying attention to my body, I have become more aware of previously unnoticed ways in which I hold tension in it. For example, I often find my hands clenched, particularly when lying in bed to sleep. Noticing this allows me to relax my hands, which immediately brings a greater sense of overall relaxation. Likewise, noticing when my shoulders are lifted towards my ears, and actively releasing them to fall in their natural position reduces feelings of tension. When approaching activities or tasks that are anxiety producing, tuning into my body and noticing how my anxiety or discomfort is being carried in my body, allows me to focus on tending to that tension first. Doing so helps to lower my anxiety before engaging in an uncomfortable activity.

Noticing your breath:

Anxiety can disrupt your breathing in a few ways. Your breath may be rapid and shallow due to sympathetic nervous system activation. You may hold your breath or "forget to breathe." Or you may find yourself chest breathing, which results in less air getting into your lungs. To notice if you are chest breathing, place your hand on your chest, then inhale and exhale. If your hand moves, you are chest breathing. Other signs of chest breathing may be frequent sighing or yawning, indicating not enough air is getting to your lungs.

By bringing awareness to your breathing throughout the day, you can engage in diaphragmatic breathing and/or the breathing exercises described in Chapter 2 to help regulate your nervous system and invite feelings of calm and relaxation. The quality of your breath cues your brain for safety or risk, and practicing diaphragmatic breathing is one of the most effective ways to cut through anxious feelings.

Moving your body to move emotion:

If your body is holding anxiety and feels jittery or charged, movement is the best way to dispel that nervous energy. Some effective movement-based interventions for anxiety are:

- Shaking your body and limbs. If you are acutely anxious, shaking your body from head to toe can serve as a release of built-up energy created by the physiological response caused by adrenaline. Animals do this in the wild after experiencing an anxiety provoking event. They shake their entire body, as if to shake off the excess energy produced but not used and to reset their nervous system
- Dancing to a favorite song can be an excellent anxiety disruptor. It combines movement with engaging in something enjoyable which also can serve as an adaptive distraction to your anxiety.

- Going for a walk or engaging in other physical activity (it does not need to be vigorous exercise) can be regulating and calming to a body that feels anxious.
- Yoga and Tai Chi are two particularly effective movement-based practices that reduce anxiety and instill feelings of calm. They are also practices that invite an inward focus, attention on the body, and the use of breath to calm and regulate.
- If your body feels stressed or has a charged, frenetic energy, this can be a cue to slow down and rest.

Ashley often experienced her anxiety as an internal "pressure cooker" and her mind "spinning like a top that is wound up." She was the mother of three young children and had a career with significant responsibilities. She often juggled multiple demands on her time and energy. When she felt this activated pressure, she often responded by pushing harder to get more done until she crashed.

I told her, "Ashley, when you feel that internal pressure and being 'wound up,' your body is telling you that it needs rest and stillness. It is communicating to you that it needs you to do less so that it can recharge, not more. And the crash you experience is what happens because you are ignoring what your body is telling you."

Ashley nodded in agreement, and said with a slight laugh, "Sometimes, in the morning, when it's crazy getting everyone ready and out of the house, I just want to lie down on the floor in my bedroom and stretch out in the sunbeam coming through the window, like my dog does."

"That! Do that! Even if only for a couple of minutes, listen to that wish your body is sending you, and give it that moment of lying in the sunbeam, where it is quiet, peaceful and still."

The more Ashley listened to her body and responded to the needs it was communicating, the more her anxiety lessened. She did let herself lie on the floor in the sunbeam. She carved out time to walk on the treadmill daily, recognizing the positive impact exercise had on her anxiety and overall sense of well-being. Sometimes, when her husband noticed her "spinning," he would offer her a long, extended hug, which always calmed her. Science tells us that a 30 second hug releases oxytocin, the "cuddle hormone", which slows heart rate, blood pressure and reduces stress and anxiety levels. When Ashley recognized her internal frenetic energy, she took it as a cue that she needed to take something off her plate, delegate, or step back in some way to quiet and still the mounting internal storm.

Another important way to think about the mind-body connection as it relates to anxiety is the concept introduced by trauma expert Bessel van der Kolk – the body keeps the score. In his book by that name, van der Kolk describes how an unhealed traumatic memory is not so much a narrative of the past, but rather a literal state of the body. In an interview in 2013 with Krista Tippet on her radio show, "On Being," van der Kolk explained this about trauma. "This is not about something you think or something you figure out. This is about your body having been reset to interpret the world as a terrifying place, and yourself as being unsafe. And it has nothing to do with cognition. You can say to people, you shouldn't feel that way, or you're not a bad person, or it wasn't your fault. And people say, I know that, but I feel that it is." (Here is that universal truth about anxiety that if you feel something to be true, you will act as if it is). What van der Kolk is speaking to is that anxiety born from trauma may not be healed without body-based interventions that transform the body's perception of safety.

Nick lived with lifelong anxiety that was often debilitating. When he was 2 years old, Nick's father was killed in a freak accident, and Nick was present and witnessed his father's death. He has no cognitive memory of the accident, but his body remembers. Throughout his life, Nick sought help with his anxiety, trying many different approaches. It was not until he started attending trauma-informed yoga classes at the age of 40 that he found meaningful relief from his anxiety. By working with his body, where the traumatic memory was stored, Nick was able to alleviate the anxiety that plagued him throughout his life.

This is not to imply that any single practice—like yoga—can fully resolve the experience of anxiety. There is an entire field called somatic therapy, which focuses on how the body holds and expresses deeply painful experiences. Somatic therapy aims to reduce the body's stress response through techniques such as mindful movement, heightened body awareness, and therapeutic touch. It is a resource to be aware of as you navigate your journey with anxiety.

True healing and relief from anxiety requires attending to both the body and the mind. If you feel stuck in your healing journey, consider whether one side of the mind-body connection has been under-attended or ignored. While this book focuses primarily on the thought and behavioral components of anxiety, be sure to incorporate body awareness into how you progress through these pages. Attending to the felt experience of anxiety in your body will yield better outcomes as you also attend to the thoughts and behaviors associated with anxiety.

Chapter 4

Anxiety Versus Intuition

I am often asked how to tell the difference between anxiety and intuition. Many people view their anxiety as an inner knowing, an internal warning system that something is not right and needs their attention. They struggle to differentiate between when their anxiety is alerting them to something that needs their attention, and when it is something to detach from, recognizing it as stories and made-up worries.

In my experience, there are observable and definable differences between the two. This likely feels different for each individual, but there are telltale signs you can look for to help you differentiate between intuition and anxiety.

Anxiety looks, sounds and feels like spinning, pressure, and intensity. It feels out of control. It is often accompanied by stories of fear and catastrophe.

Intuition is grounded, calm and still. It often appears as an internal knowing or certainty, with no judgment or story attached to it. You may feel discomfort about the knowing revealed by your intuition, but the knowing itself is quiet and comes from within. Anxiety is loud and noisy; intuition is the quiet knowing beneath the noise.

Mary suffered from severe and persistent health anxiety. This stemmed from past medical trauma in which she greatly suffered from a medical condition that went undiagnosed and untreated for years and was often dismissed as anxiety. When it was finally correctly diagnosed, Mary underwent many difficult treatments to restore some relative quality of life. What resulted from this was a hyper attunement to how she felt (always scanning her body and looking for signs of something being wrong) and a tendency to assume the worst-case scenario when she detected something that didn't feel right.

As we worked on her anxiety, Mary would often say to me, "But I do feel like something is wrong. I know something is wrong. How can I tell the difference between something that could be real, and me being anxious?"

"I can tell because there is a difference in how you talk about it when you are telling me a truth and when you are spinning in anxiety," I'd say.

Mary often responded, "Well, I am glad that you can tell the difference!" and then declared that she could not. She could not distinguish between the two - it all felt the same to her.

What I reflected to Mary was that each time she said, "Something is not right. I don't feel right", it was said as a statement. It had certainty attached to it.

When she was speaking from anxiety, her words came faster, there was pressure behind them, and there was always a story attached. "What if something really bad is wrong and I need surgery again?" "What if it's something terrible that can't be fixed?"

The statement, "Something is not right. I don't feel right," was the inner knowing, the intuition. The anxiety was all the imagined stories of what that might be. The work with Mary was to trust her intuition and disengage from the stories.

Eventually, Mary did learn she was right. By trusting her intuition and pursuing with her doctor the feeling that "something was not right," Mary caught, in its early stages, a chronic and progressive disease process.

Elaine was in treatment for obsessive compulsive disorder (OCD). Elaine's OCD would cause her to spin in anxiety, always about a made-up fear which she both obsessively thought about and compulsively responded to. The content of her specific OCD fears would shift and change. At one point, the OCD fear gripping Elaine was that she was an alcoholic. She was not. She would obsessively worry about being an alcoholic and then engage in compulsive behaviors such as taking online quizzes to determine if she was an alcoholic, reading articles in an attempt to discern if she fit alcoholic patterns, and seeking others opinions about her alcohol use – all while never feeling reassured by their responses.

In one session, Elaine was spinning in anxiety, telling me all the reasons why she feared she was an alcoholic. Like Mary, there were a lot of "what if" stories attached to her reasoning, and there was a pressured quality to her speech.

"Elaine, what I am hearing you tell me is that every person you have asked, all people who are with you when you drink, has told you they are not concerned about your drinking or see it as a problem. And yet, you keep doubting them and yourself, which is a clear sign this is an OCD fear, not reality."

"But what if I am not being honest with you or anyone else, and it really is a problem? Or what if they are all just trying to be nice because they don't want me to feel bad? What if I stop worrying about this, and then I start having trouble controlling my drinking?"

During this discussion, Elaine told me about a conversation she and her husband had in which they both concluded there were changes they wanted to make around their habits when going out. Unlike their friends who went home when they were tired, they stayed out as late as possible, a carryover from their 20s. The times when Elaine did drink more than she wanted to often happened late at night. Elaine and her husband decided it was time to "act their age" and go home earlier.

As Elaine described this conversation, she was calm and matter of fact. I asked Elaine to stop and reflect on how she was feeling, and she reported feeling calm and grounded. I observed to her that when she was telling me something that was true about her behavior and patterns around drinking, she was calm and grounded, unlike how she felt and spoke when she was caught up in the story and fears of "What if I'm an alcoholic."

There is a solidness to intuition and knowing. It is felt deep within. It does not need stories to justify its existence.

Robin Pollak, author of the book *Trust Your Intuition*, had this to say when I asked her how she would describe the difference between anxiety and intuition. "When it is fear based, it is not intuition." She went on to say that intuition does not only show up to warn you or when you are in fear. It is always present. If you don't know what your intuition feels like at other times - like when you are choosing between vanilla and chocolate or what you need in order to have a peaceful day – then you don't have enough of a relationship with your intuitive self to assume or trust that it is what is speaking to you when you are in fear. Until you have enough of a relationship with your intuition to perceive it in all the ways it shows up for you, you don't know it well enough to recognize it. Therefore, if you are only attributing intuition to fearful moments, then it is in fact your anxiety seeking to convince you by co-opting intuition to create self-doubt.

Chapter 5

Is All Anxiety Bad?

It was the very early days of the pandemic, and Lucy's husband contracted Covid. As he became progressively sicker at home, she took him to urgent care, where, alarmed by his blood oxygen level, the doctor instructed her to take him immediately to the emergency room.

Barred from entering the hospital with him, she dropped him off at the ER entrance, not knowing what would happen to him. Would he be put on a ventilator? Would he die? Lucy's husband spent 14 days in the hospital. She was not permitted to visit him. Lucy described feeling intense anxiety, unlike any she had ever known before. She was unable to sleep through the night. She feared her husband would die and she would have to raise their children alone. She spent days anxiously trying to reach overworked hospital staff for updates and panicking when she couldn't get through to anyone.

Anxiety is an appropriate response when you are in a dangerous or frightening situation or when there are high stakes attached to an outcome. In such circumstances, it is neither something to pathologize nor a problem to fix. Lucy's anxiety was both understandable and appropriate. While the tools in this book can be applied to any anxiety to bring relief, I want to emphasize that anxiety can be an appropriate response and a wise emotion.

Anxiety can also be an adaptive and useful reaction when it is responding in a proportionate way to a real rather than perceived threat. If you are walking alone at night in dark or unfamiliar surroundings, anxiety will put you on alert to fully attend to your environment and signs of danger. If you are feeling anxious about how you will do on an important exam, you can use that energy to study. If you are feeling anxious about climate change and its impact, you can channel your anxiety into actions that help address the issue, rather than remaining passive. It is important that anxiety not always be labeled as "bad", with the goal of fully eliminating it.

While the focus of this book is to lessen the pain that anxiety causes in your life, it is important to note that no feeling is bad or wrong. It just is. Feelings serve an important purpose and may have a message for you. It is not useful to bypass any feeling, including anxiety. Meeting all feelings with curiosity about what they are trying to tell you is an important emotion regulation skill. There is important information for you in your feelings.

What might your anxiety be trying to warn you about? What is it trying to tell you? How is it trying to protect you? This is not to say that it is doing so effectively or that your anxiety is telling you the truth; generally, it is not. At best, anxiety thoughts are stories. At worst, they are lies. And often, they are both. But there may be something for you to learn from your anxiety.

See if you can look beneath the content of your anxious thoughts and be curious if the feeling itself has a message for you. Is there something in your life circumstance that is no longer working for you? Is there something that you may wish to pursue or change for your greater good – even if doing so feels overwhelming or will push you outside of your comfort zone?

Often, anxiety can be an adaptive response to trauma or to an unmet need. You may have internalized a message that the world is unsafe, and you must always be on high alert to ensure your protection. You may have grown up with chaos and unpredictability, and as a means of coping, you seek predictability and order. You may have received messages, directly or indirectly, from your primary caregivers or peers that some aspect of yourself was problematic or undesirable and seek to disavow or compensate for that part of yourself. Something in your life experience may have led you to believe that uncertainty means danger. The more you understand the purpose your anxiety is seeking to serve and how it is trying to protect you, the more effectively you will be able to replace anxiety with something that is more adaptive, and that better meets the need seeking to be fulfilled. And the more curiosity and openness you bring to the feelings, not the content, the better you can discern the message or meaning the feeling might carry.

David was preparing for his upcoming wedding to Sarah. David and Sarah had dated for years and had lived together for two years before getting married. They had successfully navigated the challenges of their shared life together, due to their open and honest communication. They were kind and supportive of one another, even when tackling difficult conversations. David felt safe and cherished with Sarah, and she was consistent and reliable. If she said she was going to do something, she did it.

In the week leading to the wedding, David became increasingly anxious. He woke up in the mornings filled with dread and anxiety, familiar feelings he had struggled with for much of his life. At first, David felt panicked about the presence of these feelings, worried they were telling him something about his decision to marry Sarah. However, with his extensive experience in dealing with anxiety, he allowed the feelings to be present and focused on understanding their underlying cause rather than getting caught up in their narrative. What he found, in his quiet reflection, was his abandonment fears rooted in his childhood experience of his parents' divorce and his mother becoming an inconsistent presence in his life after the divorce.

Recognizing the feelings of anxiety as a reflexive protective stance that was attached to this history, not his relationship with Sarah, helped him to detach from them. It also allowed him to develop a deeper appreciation for the stability he found in his relationship with Sarah.

Within each of the antidotes to anxiety, I will provide you with questions to help you to better know and understand your anxiety. Curiosity and reflection will be useful tools in your journey throughout the remaining chapters of this book.

As you read about each of the three root causes of anxiety and their antidotes, allow yourself to be flexible about how you apply the suggested interventions. If a strategy recommended for one root cause of anxiety feels useful to you as you navigate anxiety stemming from a different one, use it. The answer to the question, "What is the best treatment for anxiety?" is always "The one that works for you." I am providing you with many tools for your anxiety toolbox and many strategies to work with (and to practice over time). Remember, no single approach works for everyone, and even the best strategies don't work all the time. Trust your understanding of yourself and your anxiety and lean into what feels right for you.

Chapter 6

The Anxiety Unpacked Model:
The Three Root Causes of Anxiety

Recalling Chapter 1, in which the biological function of anxiety was described, chronic and persistent anxiety is the result of habitual and often unconscious patterns of perceiving danger that is not there.

There are three primary ways in which this perception of danger manifests. These represent and form the three root causes or types of anxiety. They are:

1. Catastrophizing
2. Control
3. Distorted Beliefs

Each has distinct qualities and underlying needs shaping the resulting anxiety. Each has its own way in which the anxiety resists change. And each has its own unique solutions.

By understanding and recognizing your anxiety type, you can then attend to it in a meaningful way by implementing the specific strategies and solutions best suited to addressing the underlying need. As you learn about each of these three anxiety types, you will likely recognize your own anxious patterns and tendencies. You may resonate with one, two or all three of them. Your anxiety habits may reflect any combination of the three.

Future Catastrophizing

"What if my headache is caused by a brain tumor, and I need surgery, become disabled or die?"

Future catastrophizing happens when you create future oriented stories of worst-case outcomes. You then engage with those stories as if they are happening now or are likely to happen.

Whenever Rob's boss spoke to him in an impatient or short tone, he would call his wife and tell her he was going to get fired, though his job security had never been threatened. Elizabeth, a highly successful businesswoman, lived with a persistent fear of losing her job and becoming homeless. Jennifer was the adoptive mother of a child from another country. When her adult son expressed interest in searching for his biological family, Jennifer feared that if pursued, she might discover that her son had not been legally given up for adoption, she would lose her rights as his mother, and her son's immigration status would be revoked - all in the absence of any basis for this fear.

When my son was 16 years old, at a time when he suffered from regular and often intense anxiety, he was a counselor in training at a sleepaway camp for 2 weeks. He was excited about being a CIT and had always had positive experiences at this camp.

The day after my parents dropped him off at camp, my son called me, distress evident in his voice, and told me he needed to come home. Worried, I asked, "Why, what is wrong?"

"I'm going to be too anxious, and I'm not going to be able to handle it." he said.

"Has anything happened? Have you been anxious?"

He went on, "I started to have a panic attack on the waterfront yesterday when I went for my swim test. But I was able to calm myself down, and the test turned out fine. But I know I'm going to get anxious again, and I'm worried that I'm not going to be able to handle it."

I acknowledged his worry, refocused him on what was true (he had been anxious and dealt with it) and then told him he needed to stay for the first week. If he still felt he needed to come home at the end of the first week, we could discuss it for week two. I reassured him that I was there for him if he needed me, and he could call me anytime.

As a mother, I worried about his emotional state. As someone familiar with anxiety, I knew that rescuing him from his discomfort was not the answer. After that phone call, I did not hear from him for the remainder of the week, which I took as a good sign.

There was a 24-hour period between weeks one and two in which the CITs had to go home. My mother picked my son up to bring him to her house for those 24 hours. On the car ride, he enthusiastically told her about what a great week he had had and the friends he had made. Knowing that he had called me at the beginning of the week, my mother sent an email as soon as she returned home to reassure me all was well.

No sooner had I finished reading that email than my son called, telling me that he had a great first week but needed to come home for week 2. When I asked him why, noting how positive his first week was, he said with worry evident in his voice, "This week was good. But next week is going to be different."

This is future catastrophizing. With the knowledge that he had in fact been fine the first week, I did not let him come home the second. And in the end, he enjoyed a successful second week as well.

Future catastrophizing is easy to spot because it almost always begins with the words *What if*. Everything that follows *What if* is a story. When catastrophizing, the story is the primary source of your anxiety, not the facts. If the story is supported by facts known to be true in the present moment, then the response you are having is not catastrophizing; it is an appropriate reaction to something real. This is what I referred to as appropriate and useful anxiety in Chapter 5.

In the earlier example of Lisa, the small business owner who avoided responding to client emails, the facts she knew were that the client was making a request, and she was going to say no. The story she made up was that the client would be mad, they would then be so angry they would write a negative Yelp review, future clients would choose not to work with her because of this Yelp review, and her business would be ruined.

None of these things were happening, nor was this imagined succession of events supported by facts.

When I pointed this out to Lisa, she'd often respond, defiantly, "But it could happen".

This is the objection raised by catastrophizing. When challenged, your anxiety will try to convince you that every possible negative outcome is worthy of your attention and worry. This is a lie your brain is telling you to keep you focused on imagined fears and therefore tethered to your anxiety.

Ultimately, this is unhelpful as there is no end to the negative outcomes you can imagine or that are *possible*. That something could happen does not make it likely that it will happen.

It is theorized that there is an evolutionary purpose to catastrophizing. Neuroscientists, in tracking the neural response to uncertainty, have found heightened activity in the amygdala. This suggests a state of hypervigilance or heightened alert to potential risks.

The human mind equates uncertainty with danger. In an attempt to minimize the potential danger, the brain constantly tries to predict what will happen next, preparing the body and mind for what will be required of it. When we were a hunter-gatherer society, the threat of venturing out into the unknown could mean facing a predator or human foe, potentially resulting in death and necessitating preparation for the worst. However, this ingrained biological propensity is often more harmful than helpful in today's society and has far outlived its evolutionary purpose.

Fortunately, as is true with all three root causes of anxiety, there are specific ways you can respond to this tendency to minimize its power and influence over your emotional well-being.

The antidote to future catastrophizing is to separate the facts you know from the stories you imagine and then focus solely on the facts. This process involves practicing mindfulness and staying present in the "now" moment. It also requires building your ability to tolerate — or even become comfortable with — uncertainty. In Chapters 7 through 15, I will provide tools to help you develop these skills.

Control

"If I don't keep the list running in my head of everything that needs to get done, something will fall through the cracks. It is easier for me to do everything myself because I can't trust anyone else to do it."

A universal truth about control is that in any given situation you encounter, there will be elements within your control and elements beyond your control.

Things that are in your control are what you think and how you choose to act or react. Things not in your control are what someone else thinks, what someone else feels, someone else's choices and actions, governmental actions, acts of nature, etc.

Where you place your focus often dictates your level of anxiety. Over-attending to what is not in your control and under-attending to what is often leads to anxiety. Focusing on someone else's choices or trying to change their feelings or actions often leads to frustration and anxiety, as you're unlikely to achieve your desired outcome. You may personalize your failure, thinking their actions relate directly to, or are motivated by you. You may get caught up in feeling like a particular situation is unfair and focus your energies on the parts of the situation you lack the power to change. You then are likely to feel disempowered and victimized. When you expend your mental, emotional, or physical energy on the things you do not have the power to change, it often leads to feelings of exhaustion, defeat, anxiety, or depression. Conversely, the energy directed towards things within your control leads to feeling empowered, resourceful and resilient, the antithesis of anxiety.

Beth was a successful professional woman with a brother who suffered from severe mental illness and cognitive limitations. The choices her brother made and the way he lived his life were both concerning and baffling to Beth. In sessions, Beth would often lament her brother's choices and detail her extensive efforts to influence him. When these efforts inevitably failed, Beth would become frustrated and angry. She repeatedly gave her brother money, always without being asked, and would then be resentful when the money did not produce the desired outcome. Beth would often become angry and agitated in sessions describing her interactions with her brother, viewing his behavior as intentionally manipulative and proof of his lack of care for her.

While always validating the concern and distress Beth felt about her brother's choices, I repeatedly redirected Beth to her own actions and choices - not her brother's - noting that she had no control over him or his choices. His limitations were repeatedly reframed as reflections of his own capacities and willingness to change, not a rejection of Beth. Her frustration and anger stemmed from trying to change something outside her control—not from her brother's desire to harm her. When she chose to send him money, not because he asked her to but because she felt worried or sorry for him, it was her choosing to do so. When Beth sought to place the responsibility for her sending money on him rather than herself by declaring he was manipulating her, I would say, "He is just telling you the facts of his life. He is not asking you to do anything about them. We don't know his intentions in sharing these facts with you. You are choosing to send him money. If you resent doing so, we need to look at your choices, not blame him for them."

This always landed as true to Beth and was a helpful reminder to refocus on her choices and actions as this was the only thing over which she had control. You may also notice in this example the universal truth of anxiety discussed in chapter 2 that in the absence of information, your mind will fill in the blanks with a story that represents your worst fear or sense of vulnerability. And that story, more so than the facts, is the source of your distress. Beth's distress was often fueled by the story of the intention to manipulate or harm her that she attached to her brother's behavior. Over time, she was able to create a new relationship with her brother in which she stepped out of the role of trying to change him, stopped assigning unknown intentions to his behavior, and found ways to be a supportive connection while accepting his limitations.

Brian was blindsided when his wife asked for a divorce after 15 years of marriage. She had not previously communicated to him that she was contemplating divorce, or that she was unhappy in the marriage. She moved quickly with the divorce process and avoided engaging in conversations about her decision to help Brian understand it. He was understandably shocked and felt deeply rejected and disregarded. This was a second marriage for both, and the thought of going through another divorce was devastating to Brian. Initially, the focus of therapy was on providing a space for him to process these feelings and to make meaning of his situation.

As therapy progressed, Brian struggled to shift his focus from his wife's actions to himself and how he was going to move forward with his life. While completely justified in his feelings about how she handled the divorce process, his entrenched focus on what was not in his control (her choices and actions) kept him stuck in feelings of victimization, depression, and anxiety.

Once Brian was able to shift his focus to what was in his control - how he wanted to respond to and who he wanted to be within his new circumstances - he began to make changes that brought contentment and feelings of empowerment to his life. He changed jobs, making a career move that was more authentically aligned for him. Brian developed new friendships and pursued previously dormant interests that were neglected because his wife had not shared or encouraged them. Over time, he created a new identity for himself, and he discovered happiness he could not experience when he was focused only on his wife and her actions.

There is another way in which anxiety manifests around the issue of control. It begins with a foundational and often unconscious belief of "I am not okay" or "It is not going to be okay". When this belief is operating underneath the surface, it can often lead to one of two (or both) coping mechanisms. The first is to try to control as much of your environment as possible. The unconscious thought behind this is "If I know what to expect, or if things happen the way I think they should or I want them to, then I will be okay."

This presents as having rigid expectations and beliefs about how things should be done, over-preparing and over-researching, and trying to influence what others think and do. It is often accompanied by an acute focus on your environment and the people in it.

When it manifests in the form of over-researching and over-preparing, there is often paralysis around decision making, fearing that you will make the "wrong decision" and, therefore, it or you will not be okay. Underneath this is an over focus on the external as your source of safety and security and an under focus on self-trust. Trust in your ability to make good decisions, to cope and adapt if the decision doesn't work out, and that you possess the internal resources to handle whatever happens.

Attempts to control one's environment are problematic for several reasons. The first has to do with the universal truth about control: there will always be things in every situation in which you have no control. This includes other people's feelings and actions. Therefore, it is impossible to ever fully or even significantly control your external environment, no matter how hard you try.

Through your efforts, you are not gaining control. You are only creating the illusion of control – and at a significant cost to yourself.

Author Elizabeth Gilbert perfectly captures this truth when she wrote "You are afraid to surrender because you don't want to lose control. But you never had control. All you had was anxiety."

The second and more important problem with this strategy is that it externalizes the conditions in which you can be okay. You are placing your well-being on factors outside of yourself – where you have little or no control.

An inescapable truth in life is that sometimes things go wrong, and bad things happen. When these inevitabilities occur, it is *you* with all your internal and external resources that enables you to react, problem-solve, and cope. When you move your sense of well-being from external factors to internal ones, trusting that no matter what happens you will figure out how to be okay, anxiety has no place to take hold.

Sue, the client I spoke of in the introduction, had anxiety stemming from attempts to control her environment. She had many rigid expectations for herself and others regarding how she cleaned her home, how she presented herself, and self-imposed demands around her work that kept her in a constant state of stress. Sue was unable to relax at home unless every dish was immediately put in the dishwasher, everything was perfectly in place, and specific chores were done daily. She had rigid beliefs about the right way to do these chores, believing everything else to be the wrong way. These were exhausting standards for her to live by.

Around work, there were certain time-consuming tasks she felt compelled to do every day because of the belief that if something went wrong, having done these tasks would make it easier for her to address the problem. Doing these tasks added to her overall feeling of stress and anxiety, as well as work overload. Rarely did she utilize these time-consuming, precautionary safeguards.

While acknowledging that these behaviors and structures had positive attributes, I helped Sue to recognize why she did them: she did not trust her life would function properly and effectively if she stopped. They, therefore, felt necessary to maintain at all costs, even when doing so caused excessive and undue stress. Like many whose anxiety stems from control, Sue did not trust her internal competencies, over-attributing her success and well-being to her anxious behaviors.

Rooted in the same underlying belief, "I am not okay" or "It will not be okay" is the second coping strategy. To anticipate everything that could go wrong and make a plan for what you will do should it happen. This looks like catastrophizing but then takes it a step further by making a plan for each potential catastrophic outcome.

Joan had a pervasive habit of anticipating things that could go wrong and creating plans for what she would do should these events occur. This was exhausting and kept her mentally and emotionally oriented towards potential problems, impacting her emotional state. By her own admission, Joan had a negative outlook on life and was often anxious. She routinely expressed frustration about her lack of energy. This fatigue, in part, was caused by her habitual pattern of anticipating problems and creating solutions to them. Doing so expended significant mental and emotional energy.

One day, Joan came to a session and cheerfully told the story of an unexpected situation she had found herself in that week. She was an educator with a long commute to school and had gone to her car in the early morning to drive to work. She found all four of her tires slashed and the car undrivable. Joan calmly ordered a tow truck. She then called her school and informed them she would be unable to come in that day. When the tow truck arrived, she rode along to a tire store where all four of her tires were replaced.

While this was happening, Joan called a friend to narrate the course of events, and her friend asked, alarmed, "You're in the tow truck with the tow truck driver? Are you sure that's safe?"

Joan laughed and said, "Oh, Dave? He and I are old friends now. He's great!"

At this point in the telling of the story, I asked Joan, "Out of curiosity, in all the plans you have made to anticipate what to do when something goes wrong, did you ever plan for all four of your tires being slashed?"

She of course, responded, "No".

I then reflected that most people finding themselves in that situation would feel, at minimum, frustrated and aggravated. And yet, she seamlessly handled it without any difficulty, and cheerfully reported it not only to me, but to a friend who was concerned about things that Joan felt completely comfortable navigating. Why? Because she was dealing with each piece of the situation as it arose and successfully assessed her next move.

While this story may seem inconsequential, the principles of what happened are relevant to any situation. Later in our work together, something significantly more consequential and rightfully upsetting happened to Joan. While she didn't cheerfully talk about it, what remained true was the bad thing that happened was not something she could have anticipated, and it was Joan's internal and external resources that effectively coped with the situation – not a preordained plan.

Those who engage in the behaviors of control, more so than any other manifestations of anxiety, are convinced their anxiety behaviors are useful and elemental to their success. This is the objection used by control; the belief that your coping strategies are the reason you are successful and therefore necessary. While it is easy for me to understand why you might believe this, the fact remains that it is not the anxiety behaviors that make you successful – it is you. It is all the qualities, skills, knowledge and abilities you possess, not your anxiety, which are the source of your success.

The coping strategies adopted in an attempt to feel in control simply do not work. Firstly, there are always a multitude of factors in any given moment over which you have no control. Secondly, no one has the power to foresee the future. Even if you can predict some aspects of what will happen, certain details will only become clear in the moment. When things go wrong - as they inevitably will - you'll have to decide how to respond and cope based on the information available at that time. Therefore, any plan created in advance will lack specific details that can only be known to you when an event happens.

I routinely ask two questions to help clients buy into the idea that this particular strategy is not useful. First, "How many times did the things you anticipated actually happen, and you used the plan you'd created in advance?"

The answer to this question is universal: "Never" or "Almost never".

Next, I ask, "When you think of the worst or most stressful things that have happened to you, were any of them things you had predicted in advance and had a plan ready for?"

The answer to this question is also universally "None" or "Almost none."

The things that we plan for are not the things that happen, and the things that happen are not the things we plan for. It is not the plans you create that enable you to cope; it is *you*.

I am not suggesting that you should abandon all advance planning and preparation. There are many things you must prepare for. If you have an upcoming exam, studying is essential. If you are preparing for a trip, arranging for travel, accommodations and purchasing tickets in advance is necessary. If you have an important work presentation, thorough preparation will set you up for success.

What I am cautioning against is planning for things that are not happening and that you have no good basis (grounded in fact) for assuming will happen.

The antidotes to anxiety stemming from control involve focusing your attention only on what is in your control while accepting what is not. The deeper work is to cultivate a greater sense of trust in yourself and to shift your sense of well-being from external factors to internal ones. Anxiety and trust cannot simultaneously coexist. When you trust yourself to be able to handle anything that happens to and around you, anxiety has no place to take hold.

Distorted Beliefs

"I can't go to class if I am late because people will look at me when I walk in and will think I am weird."

A distorted belief is when you believe something negative to be true that is in fact false. Beliefs can be distorted in both positive and negative ways, but those that manifest as anxiety will always be negative beliefs. While you may have negatively distorted beliefs about the world or others, anxiety most often stems from a negatively distorted belief about *yourself*. It is like looking in a funhouse mirror and believing the image you see reflected back is an accurate representation of you.

Common negatively distorted self-beliefs that lead to anxiety are: I am unlovable, I am fundamentally flawed, I am a failure, I am worthless, I am stupid, I am unimportant, I am an outsider, I don't fit in, I'm an imposter and I am not good enough.

For some, the distorted belief is accepted and internalized as completely true. Others may know logically that the thought is untrue but feel as if it is true. As long as you feel that something is true, you will act as if it is. But even if you are stuck in this feeling, there is a way out.

Beyond impacting how you feel, distorted beliefs always lead to conscious or unconscious adaptive behaviors that either compensate for or seek to conceal the false belief. For example, if you believe you are a failure, you are likely to be afraid to try new things or pursue goals because you are certain you will fail. Many people who believe they are unlovable or fundamentally flawed often say yes to everything others want to do while never asking for anything they need or want for themselves. People pleasing becomes an attempt to feel loved and valued.

Leah had deeply ingrained patterns of behavior that reflected the strong distorted belief: "I am unlovable". She said yes to every request, even if she did not want to or if it caused significant inconvenience to her. To say no, she felt compelled to create explanations or stories to justify it, rather than simply declining. When out to dinner with friends, she frequently offered to pick up the bill for everyone, believing it was expected of her and the reason people wanted to spend time with her. If someone gave her a gift or did something nice for her, she felt compelled to respond with something even grander, unable to accept the gift or kind gesture as a demonstration of her importance or value to the giver.

Kelly held the distorted belief that others were constantly judging her and finding her to be "weird" or "awkward." These beliefs impacted her behavior daily. Examples include rehearsing what she would say to the barista at Starbucks, thinking through how she would enter a room and greet each person, and sitting in the back of church at Sunday services to avoid interacting with anyone. These beliefs were extreme distortions because Kelly was socially adept and easy to like. Her belief affected her behavior in small, unconscious ways and bigger and more painful ways as she avoided any unfamiliar social situation, including dating.

Because a distorted belief is something you perceive as true when it isn't, the world around you will inevitably provide feedback that contradicts it. The more attached to the distorted belief you are, the more sophisticated you will be in deflecting or discrediting feedback and objective evidence that reflects the truth. This is the objection used by distorted beliefs to preserve themselves.

When faced with feedback or evidence that challenges your distorted belief, you can accept and internalize the feedback, which would force you to reconsider the distorted belief or find a way to discredit it so that you can maintain the false belief. You may dismiss a compliment as being insincere or discredit the source. You may downplay your own accomplishment by asserting, "Anyone can do this, it's easy." You may deflect positive feedback by thinking, "They are just trying to be nice," "They don't want to hurt my feelings," or "They say that to everyone – they are just a nice person."

Sally had a deep attachment to the distorted belief "I am a failure." She viewed every job and life event through this lens, though it was evident that she had not failed at any of the things she claimed.

During one of our sessions, Sally told me that she had been in therapy while in graduate school at an Ivy League caliber institution many years prior. She shared that the focus of her therapy at that time was her constant fear that she was going to fail out of school at any moment.

"I am curious. When you were in graduate school, what kinds of grades did you get?"

"I got all A's?"

"Then how did you convince yourself that you were going to fail out of school?"

"Everyone in graduate school gets A's."

Not only is this not true, but it certainly was not true at this institution. This is an example of discrediting objective evidence to maintain a false belief.

Amy believed that there was something fundamentally wrong with her that made her an outsider and always on the fringe of friendships and acceptance. Yet, when I interacted with her, she was easily likable. She was kind, thoughtful, smart, and talented.

At the same time, it was true that she did not have a strong friend network. I often wondered what came first, a bit of a chicken or the egg question; her difficulty making and maintaining friendships or her belief that she was incapable, creating an obstacle to forming friendships?

This question seemed to be partially answered when Amy shared a story about being invited to a holiday party by a friend from a larger friend group. She was surprised to receive the invitation. When a friend later asked for a ride to the party, she convinced herself she had only been invited to provide transportation. Unknowingly, Amy created this narrative to reinforce her belief that she was an outsider, even though the invitation suggested otherwise. By believing this story, Amy's anxiety about attending the party became more intense.

Distorted beliefs not only affect how you feel, but also greatly impact your behaviors and ways of being in the world. The more attached to a distorted belief you are, the harder you will fight to maintain it in the face of evidence that reveals the truth.

These all become areas of work when seeking to reduce or eliminate the anxiety that stems from distorted beliefs. The antidotes to this root cause of anxiety are to identify and replace the faulty core belief, identify the behaviors that stem from the faulty belief and replace them with new behaviors that are more adaptive and reflect what is accurately true, and to learn to accept and internalize feedback that reflects the truth of who you are. It is also to practice treating yourself with kindness and self-compassion to replace the self-judgment and loathing that often accompanies distorted beliefs. This is slow and deep work that can be life changing.

The Antidotes
to Future Catastrophizing

Chapter 7

Fact Versus Fiction

Future catastrophizing is when your mind imagines the worst possible outcomes without any real evidence to support them. It usually begins with the words *What if* and everything that follows *What if* is a story. The antidotes to catastrophizing can be distilled down to two things: to be present to what is and to develop a tolerance for uncertainty.

To combat the anxiety that is caused by future catastrophizing, you must shift your focus from *what if* to *what is*. Remember, the story creating part of your brain is automatic and highly convincing, which can make it difficult to distinguish story from fact.

If you're feeling anxious about a particular situation, write down the answers to these questions on a piece of paper.

- Around this situation, what are all the things I am afraid of/worried about?
- What about this situation do I know to be true? What are the facts?

- What stories am I creating?
- Which of my fears/worries do I know will happen based on the information available to me right now
- Which of my fears/worries are based on stories of what could happen?

Writing down your answers will likely make it easier to notice the leaps in logic that may be present in your thoughts and to separate the stories from the facts.

After you have separated fact from fiction, the next step is to detach from the story and focus solely on what you know to be true. This is a practice of attending only to what is, and being in the present moment, avoiding preoccupation with the future. This is not a natural state for the human mind and one that requires practice and repetition.

Sharon lived in a state of near constant anxiety, all stemming from catastrophizing. In one session, she was feeling highly anxious about an upcoming road trip planned with a friend to attend a concert. Her anxiety about the trip was consuming her thoughts and interfering with her sleep. When I asked Sharon what about the trip was causing her to feel anxious, she told me her friend liked to smoke marijuana, particularly at concerts (this road trip was taking place at a time when marijuana was illegal in most states).

She went on to say, "What if my friend packs marijuana in her luggage? And what if, while we are driving, we get pulled over by the police? And what if they ask to search the vehicle and find the marijuana in the luggage? I keep imagining us getting arrested and ending up in jail if we go on this trip."

To Sharon, the fear that going on the road trip with her friend would lead to her being arrested and jailed seemed completely justified and valid. Her anxiety about the trip had her trapped in a state of rumination, wondering if she should cancel the trip. She was on the verge of doing so when she came to her session.

Not knowing if this fear was based on a life experience that she or others close to her had encountered, I first had curiosity about this.

"Sharon, has something like that ever happened to you or someone you know?"

"No"

"So, there is nothing specific in your life experience that informs this fear?"

"No. But she does like to smoke pot so that is a given."

"Okay, so that part of this fear is based in fact. You know that she likes to smoke pot and your experience with her tells you that she is likely to want to on this trip. How do you feel about that?"

"I am not comfortable with it. I don't care if she smokes at the concert, but I don't want her to bring anything with her in the car."

"That's important. You have a clear sense of what you're not comfortable with. Have you expressed this to her?"

"No, I haven't."

"How would you feel about going on the trip with her if she didn't bring marijuana?"

"I would be fine with that!"

"Have you considered telling her how you feel about this and asking her not to bring it with her on the trip?"

Sharon thought about this for a moment, a look of dawning awareness on her face.

"No! Somehow, I never thought of that."

"Let's consider telling her you do not want her to bring marijuana on the trip." I paused allowing her to sit with this thought for a moment.

"And now, when you think about going on this trip with her, with this boundary in place, how do you feel?"

Sharon paused and reflected, then said, "I feel good."

"Any anxiety?"

"No - no anxiety."

Sharon shared her unease about traveling with marijuana with her friend, who readily agreed to travel without it. Sharon experienced no further anxiety, and they went on the trip as planned. Reflecting on the experience, Sharon said the trip was a great time for her and her friend, and everything about it had been smooth and easy. She appreciated having communicated her needs instead of canceling the trip and gained greater insight into her relational patterns through exploration of why she had not considered this to be an option on her own.

Sharon's story highlights the paralysis around decision making that often accompanies future catastrophizing. When your mind automatically imagines catastrophic outcomes, it becomes difficult to make decisions about how to proceed because your mind perceives danger at every decision point. And every perceived danger can feel like a likely outcome worth weighing.

Catastrophizing is also likely to impact the decisions you make. If your mind is desperately warning you of potential bad outcomes and problems, it is only natural that you will seek to avoid them.

Generally speaking, decisions made from unfounded fears will not be good ones. When you make decisions based on *What if's*, there is a greater likelihood you will regret them. Your best decisions will be ones made in connection with your authentic self and feelings, as well as the information available in the moment.

This is referred to in dialectical behavioral therapy (DBT) as the *Wise Mind*.

Wise Mind is a concept that describes three different states of mind and the place from which decisions are made in each state. The three states are:

- Emotional Mind - driven by feelings
- Logical Mind- driven by logic
- Wise Mind - a middle ground between the two.

This graphic illustrates the Venn diagram of these three states and the place from which our best decisions are made.

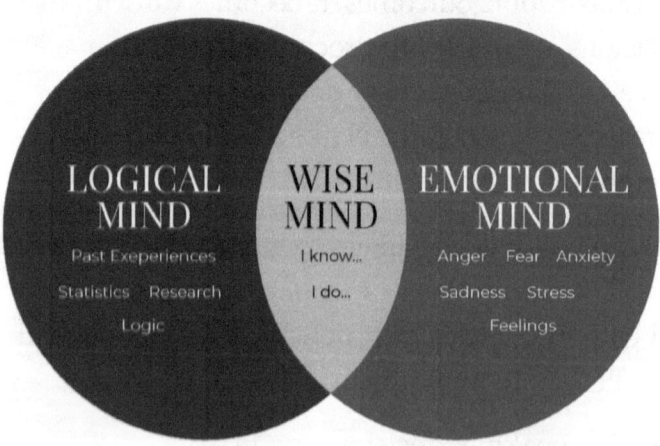

In Sharon's story, her anxiety was partly based on an authentic feeling that was important to pay attention to; she was not comfortable driving across the country with her friend if she brought illegal substances. The catastrophizing part of her mind magnified the danger of this by creating a story of being pulled over by the police, having the vehicle searched, being arrested, and going to jail. When contemplating the trip, Sharon ignored her authentic feelings by not allowing herself to set a boundary with her friend. Sharon then became trapped in the catastrophe story, likely in part because she was ignoring a true concern. When she was able to acknowledge the genuine discomfort and refocus on what she knew to be true about the situation, she was able to come to a decision that reflected her wise mind.

Many people, like Sharon, feel completely attached to their stories and see them as valid and reasonable things to worry about. They will often say, if challenged, "It could happen!" Anything could happen. If this is the primary rationale for clinging to your fear, it is not a real fear and nothing more than a story your mind is creating. Others recognize that their story is irrational but cannot detach from the anxious feelings associated with the story. The goal is always to detach from the story and to tolerate the uncomfortable feelings. Mindfulness can be a useful tool to help you achieve this goal.

Chapter 8

Mindfulness:
Your Compass to the Present Moment

Mindfulness is the practice of intentionally focusing your attention on the present moment with curiosity, openness and without judgment. The goal of mindfulness is not to achieve an "empty mind" or to eliminate thought; it is simply to observe your thoughts and feelings without attaching to them or judging them. You may think of your thoughts as clouds passing by as they move across the sky, a leaf being carried down the stream by a gentle current, or a balloon that is drifting away. If your thoughts feel more persistent and attention seeking, you may try viewing them as rain clouds or a thunderstorm that, while perhaps undesired, will eventually pass. Just as clouds, rain and thunderstorms represent the shifting nature of feelings and emotions, you represent the sky - the constant- not the weather that appears from day to day.

Byron Katie, the author *of Loving What Is* captured the essence of mindfulness when she wrote, "Thoughts are just what is. They appear. They are innocent.

They're not personal. They're like the breeze or the leaves on the trees or the raindrops falling. Thoughts arise like that, and we can make friends with them. Would you argue with a raindrop?"

Another way to think of this is that you have thoughts, but you are not your thoughts. You have feelings, but you are not your feelings. Understanding this separation allows you to detach more easily from your thoughts and feelings without giving them more power than is warranted. Moreover, thoughts and feelings are not facts. They are real, but thinking and feeling something does not make it true. It is important to remember that anxious thoughts are rarely true.

Mindfulness helps you to become more aware of your body and physical manifestations of anxiety. By creating a mindfulness practice, you will become more attuned to your body and more readily notice physical sensations that signal or trigger anxiety. This will help you to implement the body centered relaxation techniques discussed in Chapter 3 that are essential to relieving anxiety.

Mindfulness is also a practice of creating a pause – of observing thoughts and feelings and pausing to intentionally choose your response. The renowned mindfulness teacher and author Sharon Salzberg says, "Mindfulness allows us to watch our thoughts, see how one thought leads to the next, decide if we're heading down an unhealthy path, and if so, let go and change directions."

Viktor E. Frankl, Holocaust survivor and the author of *Man's Search for Meaning*, said, "Between stimulus and response, there is a space. In that space is our power to choose our response. In our response lies our growth and our freedom." Pausing to choose your response allows you to break free of habitual patterns or unconscious responses to thoughts and feelings that may not be serving you and your greater good.

Laurie grew up in a chaotic home environment in which her father had a violent and explosive temper. When his rage was triggered, which happened easily and often, he became violent towards her, her siblings and her mother. Her father was also belittling and verbally abusive. Laurie described being terrified of her father but also combative in response to his anger. Though she avoided her father's wrath as a child, when she became a teenager, she fought back against him.

As an adult, Laurie replicated some of her father's explosive reactions. Though never physically violent, she was quick to temper outbursts and would easily become enraged at others. This created turmoil in her family relationships and in her workplace. When triggered into anger, Laurie was quick to blame others.

Laurie began therapy shortly after her divorce from her wife, who left the marriage because of Laurie's volatile temper. In her more reflective moments, Laurie recognized that her behavior was damaging to herself and those she loved. She came to understand her reactions as an adaptive response to her father's temper, attempting to protect her and keep her safe but ultimately recreating the behavior she was seeking to protect herself from. Yet, at the outset of therapy, she was convinced that she was unable to control her reactions, as their onset was sudden and automatic, and often in response to external triggers that she saw as justifying her reactions.

Laurie's behavior transformed significantly through mindfulness practices and by committing to a daily meditation practice. She learned to become more attuned to both her feelings and accompanying physical sensations in her body so she could catch herself escalating, even if only a moment before erupting. She learned to implement a pause – a brief moment between having a feeling and reacting to that feeling. Within the pause, she engaged in breathing and relaxation techniques such as counting or repeating soothing mantras, creating enough space to choose a new response. She learned the difference between having a feeling, which was always accepted for what it was, and having a reaction to that feeling, which she chose with more intention.

One way of practicing mindfulness is to set aside time to be an observer of whatever thoughts, feelings and sensations are present without attaching or reacting to them. It can be aided by closing your eyes, and paying attention to your breath, noticing your lungs breathing in and out. As you focus on the rhythm of your breath, notice any sensations in your body, and just observe them. You will also notice thoughts coming into your mind. You can observe these thoughts, and let them pass by, returning your focus to your breath so as not to attach to them. You may use an observational voice such as, "I am noticing myself thinking about work", or "I notice that I am feeling sad." To any thoughts or feelings that arise, you can identify them as "that is just a thought I am thinking" or "that is just a feeling I am feeling." You want to do this from a stance that no thought or feeling is good or bad; it just is.

Mindfulness helps you to remain focused on the present moment, which keeps you from future-oriented stories and worries. It can be particularly useful for those who know their stories are irrational but feel impacted by them, nonetheless.

The act of noticing thoughts and worries, without feeling the need to attend to them, helps create freedom from anxiety. It is the difference between standing in the ocean, repeatedly getting knocked down by powerful and bruising waves or standing away from the water, watching the waves come crashing in, but not being touched by them. The more you consistently practice mindfulness, the more quickly it can be used as a tool to move from a state of anxiety to a state of calm.

Significant research has validated the benefits of mindfulness on emotional and cognitive health. These benefits include:

- Reduced rumination

93

- Increased positive effect and decreased negative affect and anxiety
- Improved working memory
- Improved focus and concentration
- Less emotional reactivity
- Greater cognitive flexibility which directly correlates with decreased anxiety and depression.

Another important benefit of mindfulness is that it allows you to connect with yourself – your true self that lies beneath the many thousands of thoughts the average person thinks in a day. When you feel anxious due to future catastrophizing, you become disconnected from the present moment, from others, and from yourself. Your thoughts, emotions, and energy are focused on a future outcome that you don't know will happen. Not only does this cause distress, but it robs you of being present in the here and now, which is where your greatest potential for well-being resides. The more you connect to yourself and others in the present moment, the greater your potential for feelings of peace, calm, and well-being.

Margot came from a highly traumatic upbringing in which there was little predictability and safety. She was exposed to physical abuse and neglect and was largely responsible for her daily care and that of her siblings, even as a young child. From the time she was young, Margot existed in a state of high alert, constantly looking for signs of danger. As an adult, Margot was prone to future catastrophizing. She automatically, often without awareness, would scan the environment, looking for signs of danger. This was an extension of a childhood coping mechanism. While she was often not safe or appropriately cared for in her childhood, as an adult, her life was secure and stable.

As Margot and I worked on her anxiety, she became increasingly aware of the ways in which her future catastrophizing kept her emotionally disconnected from the safe, stable, and secure life she had created. One day, Margot came to a session and described an experience she had while out on her daily walk. She practiced being present to what she experienced on her walk, rather than being consumed with worries or searching for signs of danger. The experience was a revelation for her. She was able to hear the birds chirping, notice the clouds moving across the sky, and feel the warmth of the sun. She saw children playing together at a playground, mothers and young children interacting with each other, and people walking their dogs. She made eye contact and smiled as she passed people on her walk. None of this was familiar or representative of her usual walks. Typically, she would either scan the environment for signs of danger, or be lost in her thoughts, worrying about tasks on her to-do list or problems needing her attention. What she noticed was how at peace and genuinely happy she felt simply by being present to the here and now, rather than consumed by her thoughts.

Suddenly, the concept of being disconnected from herself and others because of her anxiety was brought to life in a tangible way. Margot was so used to her state of anxiety that she had no perspective or frame of reference for what it looked or felt like to be absent from it. The experience on her walk gave her a taste for what was possible.

In this example, the here and now was safe and free from anxiety or distress. However, there will be times when the present moment may include stressful circumstances or uncomfortable feelings. When this is the case, you still want to evaluate if the distress is attached to something true and real, or a story. Even in the presence of distressing realities, practicing observing your thoughts and feelings without judgment may change the way you relate to what is. Being present and knowing that any thought or feeling is temporary, as is any situation you find yourself in, may help you to tolerate the feeling. Breathing to calm and regulate your nervous system will help you to remain more connected to self, and a sense of safety.

If there is something in your present moment that is distressing, can you identify other things that are also true that may serve as a cushion or buffer? Might you recognize that you have been in similar situations before and successfully navigated them? Can you notice you have support around you and are not alone? Could it be true that while a particular circumstance may be stressful or concerning, you possess the ability to cope?

These are all ways you can be present with what is, while remaining detached from and avoiding the trap of catastrophizing.

And of course, if what is is truly distressing, unsafe, or problematic, it is always important to normalize your feelings and reactions with compassion and non-judgment. Remember, if anxiety is appropriate to true problems or unsafe circumstances, it is not problematic and may in fact be helpful and useful.

Mindfulness requires intentionality and practice. Though you will derive some benefit from any amount of time spent practicing mindfulness, research suggests that spending 20 minutes a day will help you achieve the optimal benefits from it.

Most people feel intimidated by the prospect of starting a mindfulness practice. For one, it is often misunderstood what this means and what it entails. Mindfulness does not require sitting in silence with an empty mind. For those who have experienced trauma, sitting quietly in a still and meditative state can feel uncomfortable or unsafe. There are many approaches to building a practice of mindfulness and many tools to help you do so. The key is to find the ones that best suit you. These include:

- Starting small and gradually building. Mindfulness is like exercise; you have to build your capacity for it. You can begin with as little as 1-2 minutes to start and then gradually increase the time you set aside to practice mindfulness.

- Mindfulness can be practiced at any time of day. There is no right or wrong time to practice.
- You can practice mindfulness while in movement or while doing an activity.

Margot practiced mindfulness while walking.

Other activities that promote mindfulness through movement are:

- swimming laps
- yoga
- running
- tai chi
- raking leaves
- gardening

Mindfulness can be practiced while doing everyday activities such as loading the dishwasher, vacuuming, folding laundry, and eating. This involves bringing your attention as fully as possible to what you are doing and/or to engage all your senses in the activity.

Being in nature is a powerful way to draw your focus and attention outside of yourself through awareness of a greater world/universe surrounding you paired with a sense of awe, wonder, or appreciation. Being in nature is both grounding and easily engages you in the present, "now" moment. It is also a soothing balm for the nervous system. The sights and sounds of nature have a calming effect, gently quieting racing thoughts and promoting a sense of peace.

Meditation apps or online videos can guide you in mindfulness practices. If sitting in silence feels uncomfortable or difficult, listening to guided practices so that your mind has something soothing to engage with may feel more comfortable.

Chapter 9

Grounding: How to Stay Present in Discomfort

If mindfulness provides awareness of the present moment without judgment, grounding is a practice to help you regulate anxiety and overwhelm by using the present moment to create a sense of safety within your body. Grounding techniques help anchor you in the here and now, particularly when you feel disconnected from yourself, caught up in future worries, or are experiencing anxiety related to past trauma that has been activated in the present moment. There are several techniques you can practice to ground yourself.

1. Tuning into your five senses with the 5-4-3-2-1 technique.

Wherever you are, focus on your environment and identify:

- Five things you can see
- Four things you can touch
- Three things you can hear
- Two things you can smell

- One thing you can taste

For example, at this moment, as I sit and write, I can see my hands moving on the keyboard, the light on my desk, my laptop, the water bottle on my desk, and the sunlight coming through the window. Four things I can feel are the keys of the keyboard, the seat of my chair, the slight chill in the room, and the carpet under my feet. Three things I can hear are the sound of the keyboard, the quiet in the room, and an electrical whir in the background. Two things I can smell are my hand lotion and lip balm. One thing I can taste is the water in my water bottle.

2. Anchor Yourself in the Room

Place your feet on the floor. Feel your feet rooted and connected to the ground. Slowly, look all around the room or your surroundings. Take in all the details. The goal here is to ground yourself in the present moment by attending to as many details as you can notice about the space you are in. Animals do this in the wild - looking around, assessing, "Am I safe here?" This is what you are seeking to achieve - a firm connection to the here and now, and a sense of safety within your immediate surroundings.

3. Focus on your breath

Noticing your lungs breathing in and out and focusing on the rhythm of your breath is both a grounding technique and a mindfulness practice. When used as a mindfulness practice, it is a way to detach from your thoughts. When used as a grounding technique, it is a way of bringing yourself into your body.

4. Butterfly Tapping

This is a technique that uses bilateral stimulation for grounding and calming your nervous system. Cross your hands over your chest so that your palms are resting on the opposite shoulder. Interlock your thumbs so that your hands form the shape of a butterfly. Alternate your hands tapping on your collar bone just below your shoulders, one hand at a time. As you tap, you can add a mantra such as:

- I am safe
- I am okay
- I am calm

Practicing these techniques when you feel overwhelmed, anxious or panicked promotes self-soothing and a sense of safety during moments of emotional distress.

Chapter 10

Collecting Positive Moments

When catastrophizing, your mind is focused on stressful or fearful thoughts and outcomes. If you recall, when the amygdala perceives danger, it triggers the mind to hyper-focus on the threat or problem so that you can better attend to it. Because of the interconnection between thoughts, feelings, and actions, your feelings will follow if you are focused on problems or danger. Add to this the fact that the human mind is wired to attend more to the negative than the positive, yet another function of your innate drive to survive, and you can see how anxiety quickly reinforces itself. A further truth is that what your mind focuses on shapes your reality. If you are focused on potential problems and worries, you'll experience more of them because your mind instinctively notices and prioritizes anything that reinforces and validates your focus. Creating practices that disrupt these patterns of focus and thought will help to lessen and counter your anxiety over time.

105

Collecting positive moments is a practice that can be effective in reducing anxiety. Training your mind to notice and dwell in positive moments will shift your feelings accordingly. And because what your mind focuses on becomes your experience, creating a practice of capturing positive moments will increase your ability to notice and feel them.

Deb Dana, an expert in the use of polyvagal theory to treat trauma, coined the term "glimmers" in her 2018 book *The Polyvagal Theory in Therapy*. Glimmers refer to small moments that spark happiness, contentment, connection or peace, which then cues your nervous system to feel safe and calm. Glimmers are not intended to be big, expansive experiences of joy but rather small moments found in your daily experience. Examples include:

1. A smile from a stranger
2. A message from a loved one or friend
3. A moment shared with a beloved pet
4. Viewing something beautiful while out for a walk
5. Hearing a favorite song

These are small moments that, when noticed and captured, help to create more regulation in your nervous system and help you to access states of calm more easily when needed.

When I was an undergraduate student, I was a TA for Psychology 101. In this role, I was required to create and run a small group experiment around a topic in psychology. I created a positive psychology experiment in which the student participants were instructed to keep a daily journal to record every positive interaction or experience they had each day during the experiment period. At the beginning of the experiment, they each rated their mood using a mood scale. They were instructed to use their journals daily for three weeks. At the end of the three weeks, they scored their mood again using the same rating scale.

This was not a rigorous scientific experiment. It was based on a very small number of subjects, and each student self- selected to sign up for this experiment. Additionally, there was no control group. Yet, each participant recorded a higher mood score at the end of the experiment than they had at the beginning.

In debriefing their experiences, each observed that the more positive interactions and experiences they recorded, the more of them they noticed. They noted that many of the items recorded in their journals were not big, meaningful moments but rather small interactions that brought a feeling of happiness or peace – glimmers. Some described their experience as becoming trained to notice more positivity. Being more attuned to positive moments, their mood was elevated. It was not that they experienced fewer negatives; it was that the positives helped create a cushion to soften the impact of the negatives. Many carried their journals with them throughout their day, and some said that looking for experiences to record in their journal became like a fun game.

Perhaps this is a game you can begin playing yourself.

Chapter 11

Gratitude: More Than What Feels Good Now

A growing body of scientific literature has found that gratitude positively affects both physical health and emotional well-being. Gratitude involves embracing all of what has contributed to your life. It places your focus not just on what is going well in the moment but also on all the factors that have contributed to anything good in your life.

Robert Emmons, the author of *The Gratitude Project: How the Science of Thankfulness Can Rewire our Brains for Resilience, Optimism and the Greater Good,* and a leading expert on the science of gratitude, defines gratitude as having two parts. The first is to affirm goodness wherever you spot it. The second is to recognize that the source of this goodness resides outside of you. This is the recognition that you receive gifts from other people, a higher power, the natural world, etc. This focus helps you to recognize that there is goodness you are always receiving, even in the midst of challenges. Emmons says about gratitude, "Practicing gratitude magnifies positive feelings more than it reduces negative feelings." This aids your resilience and ability to cope with challenges.

Nancy Davis Kho, author of the book *The Thank-You Project: Cultivating Happiness One Letter of Gratitude at a Time* explains that strengthening your positive recall bias makes it easier to see the good things around you when times are dark. To commemorate her 50th birthday, Nancy set out to write 50 thank-you letters to people in her life who helped shape the person she had become or who had inspired her. At first, she struggled to come up with a list of 50 people; however, once she started, not only did her ability to identify recipients of these letters grow, but she also found the practice naturally boosted her positive emotions. The act of writing thank you letters strengthened her positive recall bias, thus more easily seeing ways she had been positively influenced and inspired and, therefore, identifying people to thank. What surprised Davis Kho was how noticing and savoring examples of goodness in her life led to a transformational experience of increased happiness. This was an unexpected byproduct of her practicing gratitude, and an emotional transformation she had not anticipated.

Because catastrophizing involves a disproportionate focus on future oriented worries and outcomes, building your ability to notice and feel positivity in the present moment is a disruptor to anxiety caused by catastrophizing.

Practicing gratitude does not ask that you minimize, discount or disregard the struggles and challenges you are facing. You can acknowledge the struggles while also noticing what is working in your life, how and by whom you are supported, and what needs are being met. Gratitude and challenges can and do exist side by side.

To help you identify potential sources of gratitude, think beyond positive experiences and notice all that has and does contribute to your well-being. This can include physical health, any amount of security you have to meet your basic needs, people who love and support you, opportunities you have been given, mentorship you have received, etc. One of my friends wakes up every morning and expresses gratitude for her comfortable bed, for heating and cooling, for running water and clean water to drink, for her lungs that are breathing, for her body that is functioning, and so on. She makes note of things that could easily be taken for granted. A client, suffering from chronic pain due to an injury, goes on daily walks and feels grateful that she is able to go for her walks, even while feeling pain.

Gratitude practices you can incorporate into your daily routine are:

1. Keeping a gratitude journal. There is no right or wrong way to do it. Some tips that might help you get started are:

- Make it a regular practice. If not daily, at least 3 times a week on an ongoing basis.
- Be specific when listing your gratitude.
- Focusing on people over things has a stronger impact, though both are valuable.
- Include surprises and unexpected positive events
- Have variety - try to find at least one new thing to include each time.
- Quality over quantity - don't get hung up on having a certain amount of gratitude. Instead, focus on anything that feels sincere, even if it is only a small number of things.

2. Write letters or notes of gratitude. Just as Nancy Davis Kho did, you can begin the practice of writing thank-you notes. These can be in the form of cards, letters, emails, or texts. There are multiple benefits to this practice. It can help increase your sense of appreciation and positivity. And sharing your gratitude with others will likely increase your sense of connection to others, which is one of the most important factors in emotional well-being. We suffer in isolation and heal and thrive in connection.

3. Gratitude Jar. This is a simple practice of writing gratitude's on a slip of paper and placing them in a jar or other container to collect positive moments of thankfulness. The jar provides a visual reminder of gratitude. In times of low

mood, you can pull out and read slips from the jar to remind yourself of the positive contributions that have been made to your life.

Noelle McWard Aquino

Chapter 12

Becoming Comfortable
with Uncertainty

Beyond being with *what is*, not *what if*, another antidote to catastrophizing is developing a tolerance for uncertainty. Author Eckhart Tolle beautifully said, "When you become comfortable with uncertainty, infinite possibilities open up in your life. It means fear is no longer a dominant factor in what you do and no longer prevents you from acting to initiate change. If uncertainty is unacceptable to you, it turns into fear. If it is perfectly acceptable, it turns into increased aliveness, alertness, and creativity."

The human mind equates uncertainty with danger. In a bid to keep you safe, your mind will assume the worst, over-personalize threats, and jump to wrong conclusions all in the name of protection. To make matters worse, you are hardwired to overestimate threats and underestimate your ability to handle them. This is part of your evolutionary design to keep you safe by steering you away from the possibility of losing something you value (pride, sense of security, money, etc.). While well intentioned, this innate protective mechanism causes more harm than good in its overzealous efforts to keep you safe. Catastrophizing is a hallmark of human discomfort with uncertainty. Anxiety behaviors associated with catastrophizing, such as ruminating, are attempts to eradicate uncertainty before taking action – an impossible state to achieve.

So, how does one become comfortable with uncertainty and achieve the state that Eckhart Tolle describes? One way is to turn uncertainty, which invites fear, into possibility, which elicits feelings of anticipation and expansiveness. What if you imagine possibility within the space of uncertainty? Possibility can include good things that might happen, opportunities that might present themselves, lessons you might learn or personal growth you might experience.

Robert suffered from health anxiety. This was the byproduct of growing up in a home where doctors were deeply mistrusted. Robert had an older sister who died at the age of 3 from a rare cancer before he was born. Robert's mother had taken his sister to doctors multiple times before the cancer was diagnosed, often with reassurances that her child was fine. This, coupled with the failure of her daughter's cancer treatment, bred deep mistrust of the medical system, which his mother routinely verbalized. Robert internalized his mother's fear and distrust of doctors and avoided the medical system for most of his life.

Robert engaged in therapy following a heart attack, which resulted in his hospitalization and undergoing emergency open heart surgery. Recognizing the need to attend to health issues and interact with the medical system for follow-up care, Robert sought help with the intense anxiety he felt in anticipation of every doctor's appointment, lab appointment, or diagnostic test. Because of his family's trauma, his default expectation was to be dismissed while also anticipating catastrophic outcomes.

To help lower his anxiety before an appointment, Robert would practice saying to himself, "It's possible this doctor will listen to me and help me", "I can have good experiences with doctors," or "I can have my own experience, different from my mother's." These were possibilities of positive outcomes that his anxiety did not naturally allow him to consider. Other times, he would tell himself, "I will be relieved to get this test done and find out that everything is okay." These statements helped lower his anxiety before visiting the doctor.

Jill was a recent college graduate applying to graduate school. Her mind would automatically jump to catastrophic stories each step of the way.

"What if I don't get a good score on the GRE?"

Then, when she got an excellent score, "What if I don't get into any of the schools I apply to?"

Then, when she was accepted at most schools she applied to, "What if I can't afford the tuition?"

Then, when she was offered financial aid, "What if when I graduate, I don't get a job that will enable me to pay back my student loans and live?"

Each time Jill experienced success, she created a new catastrophic story that paralyzed her as fear led to inaction and avoidance. She would fall into procrastination and even considered giving up on going to graduate school altogether.

And each time I would ask her, "How would it feel if you succeeded? Let's imagine for a moment that you will get a good score (or get into schools you are excited about, get financial aid, or find a way to pay for graduate school and repay your loans). How would you feel then?"

By imagining what was possible, Jill felt excited and calmer. This then gave her access to the more rational part of herself that could objectively look at her strengths and qualifications, as well as her problem-solving skills around potential bad outcomes. This enabled her to move forward step by step. She went on to attend a prestigious graduate school, secured financial aid, worked part-time while in graduate school to lessen the shortfall, and secured a job post-graduation working for an organization she had long admired.

Take out a piece of paper. Draw a line down the center of the page. On one side of the page, write down anything that you are avoiding or feeling anxious about because you are projecting into uncertainty, fear or potential problems.

Next, consider what good outcomes might be possible for each thing you have written down. Write these down on the other side of the paper next to the corresponding item on your list. Sit for a moment in these possibilities and notice how you feel.

Finally, recognize that worry and avoidance cannot create certainty where uncertainty exists. You can't know what will happen or what will be revealed or unfold over time. Many who suffer from anxiety feel paralyzed in making decisions or taking action until the unknown is known. This also leads to rumination, as the mind seeks to eliminate uncertainty through overthinking (believing the answer can be found in your thoughts). This is impossible. You cannot know the unknowable, and you don't need to. You only need to know what is right in front of you and what the next step is. As you take each step, new information will become available to you, and you will decide your next move based on what has been revealed. Think of it like taking a walk in the dark with a flashlight. Only the ground directly in front of you is illuminated. But by taking each step forward, the new ground will become visible, leading you step by step to your destination.

Look at your list of possibilities, the counterparts to your avoidance. Choose one thing on the list you want to step into action around. In considering taking action, identify what would be the first step you would take - only the first step. Within the feeling of possibility, commit to taking that one step. Then take it. Based on the outcome of that one step and the information revealed to you, consider what your next step is. Commit to taking that step and then act. Then repeat.

A final tool for building comfort with uncertainty is to focus on what you do know. By this, I mean not only the facts, but also your truth. You may notice when making decisions that your mind gravitates towards all the things you don't want rather than what you do want. This again is a function of your brain's quest for safety. In these moments, your brain is concerned with your safety, not your happiness. It can be helpful to refocus on what you do want, the values you wish to embody, your goals and priorities – and then base your decision making on this. Questions you might ask to help you refocus are:

- What do I know I want?
- What values do I wish to express through my choice/decision?
- What things, related to this decision, are important to me?
- What is my goal?
- What is my ideal outcome?

Then, consider what next step or option in front of you best aligns with what you know you want. The outcomes that are outside your control or beyond your knowing are not where you want to place your attention. There is no amount of thinking that will make the unknowable knowable, nor what is beyond your control controllable. Focus instead on the next step that takes you towards your goal, or an action that aligns with your values. And remember that you can take steps towards your goals and values while feeling discomfort. You do not need to be free of anxiety and worry to move forward. When stepping outside your comfort zone, you can be uncomfortable and take action that moves you towards your desires and goals at the same time. If it is something you wish to do and you feel scared, do it scared.

Chapter 13

Befriending Your Anxiety

A final strategy that can be useful with catastrophizing is to make friends with your anxiety. Catastrophizing is fear based. It is like a car alarm going off, warning you of danger. Anxiety is an unpleasant and uncomfortable feeling, and one often viewed as an enemy. It can be useful to think of your anxiety as a friend (albeit a misguided one) trying to help and protect you.

Robert recognized that his anxiety was trying to protect him from repeating the trauma his mother had experienced with the medical system. It was trying to keep him safe, based on what he had internalized about doctors from his mother. The problem was that his anxiety could not differentiate between the past, rooted in a specific experience his mother had many decades before, and his present realities and experiences with doctors.

A turning point for Robert came when he stopped fighting his anxiety and being critical of himself for feeling it and thanked it for trying to help him. He went a step further and gave his anxiety a name and a persona. Initially, he saw his anxiety as a dark force, much like Voldemort from the Harry Potter books. When the anxiety emerged, he would speak to it by name (borrowing the phrase "He who shall not be named") and have conversations with it, sometimes appreciative of its efforts, misguided as they were, and sometimes humorous.

The more Robert communicated with his anxiety in this way, the more his relationship with his anxiety shifted to one of greater compassion and appreciation. Over time, Robert decided that Voldemort was no longer the right personification of his anxiety because his stance towards it had softened. He began to see it instead as a small, hyperactive dog, barking anxiously to keep danger away like an overzealous guard dog. He began responding to his anxiety as he would this guard dog, kindly acknowledging its efforts and reassuring it that all was well, and its protection was not needed.

One day, at an art fair, Robert purchased a small painting of a dog that looked like his imagined guard dog. He moved the painting from room to room to create a visual reminder and representation of his anxiety. He sometimes would give his guard dog a job to do so that it would feel useful. Robert and I laughed together one day as he shared that he had printed out his most recent blood work results and placed them in front of the painting so that "Petey the guard dog" could study them and be reminded that Robert was healthy. And while appreciating the creativity and sense of fun he was having with "Petey," I also noted how this approach had brilliantly transformed Robert's relationship with his anxiety. What once was something to fear was now something he could good humoredly appreciate and be in relationship with rather than in conflict with.

Kelly had a successful career as an attorney with a major law firm and was on track to becoming a partner. Kelly's anxiety was noticeably heightened when she was recognized in a positive way. If she was praised at work, rewarded with more complex cases or high-profile clients, or made advancements towards becoming a partner, the *What if* scenarios of failure or being revealed as a fraud took over. These *What if* fears felt real, compelling, and disruptive, often causing Kelly significant distress. Her typical response was to challenge them, which often found her in a cycle of battling her anxious thoughts. The more she sought to challenge and defuse them, the harder they seemed to fight back with new scenarios of her being revealed as a fraud. This was an exhausting and often repeated pattern.

Through exploration of when these fears began and what they were seeking to protect her from, Kelly remembered being as young as 5 and paralyzed with the same fears. She connected the fear to her early struggles with reading. In spite of support from her parents and teachers, she struggled during "read aloud" time in kindergarten, more so than her classmates. And in later grades, no matter how much she prepared for vocabulary tests, she was never able to finish them in the allotted time. Though her reading ability eventually caught up with and at times exceeded that of her peers, Kelly's anxiety over being revealed as insufficient never left her.

Once this connection was made, Kelly was asked to reflect on how her anxiety was seeking to help and protect her; viewing it through the lens of her five-year-old self who struggled to read as well as her classmates and who felt self-conscious, exposed, and inadequate as a result. Kelly connected with the worry that if she saw herself as deserving of the praise and opportunities she was given, she might not work as hard as she did now. This then might expose her to the same feelings of shame and embarrassment she had felt as a young girl when she couldn't read as well as her peers. She saw that her anxiety was trying to protect her by making her work harder to avoid being found lacking in any way. Understanding this about her anxiety helped her to feel more compassion for herself, and for her anxiety's good intentions.

A turning point for Kelly came when she started to consider how she could view her and her anxiety as on the same team, rather than something she needed to constantly battle and challenge. Whenever I reminded Kelly that her anxiety was trying to take care of her 5-

year-old self, the best way it knew how, she felt herself soften towards it. And then, from this place, she was better able to respond to her anxiety in a way that appreciated and reassured it rather than fighting against it. Over time, she found that her fear of being revealed as a fraud lessened and she was more easily able to embrace her capabilities and competence.

Now it is your turn. Think about common scenarios in which your anxiety emerges or common themes for your anxious thoughts. Then, ask your anxiety:

- What are you trying to protect me from? Look beyond the content of your thoughts and seek to find a theme unifying them.
- How are you trying to help me?
- What are you afraid will happen if I don't have anxiety in this situation?
- When do I first remember having this fear?
- What experience (s) have I had that informs this fear?

Write down whatever answers come to you.

Once you connect with what your anxiety is seeking to protect you from, you can thank it for trying to keep you safe. Some questions about your anxiety you may then want to consider are:

- Is there a way we can work together to address your concerns in a more constructive manner?
- Do you have any positive intentions for me?

When you reflect on your first memories of this anxiety, ask yourself these questions:

- What is different now from what was true in the situation when this anxiety emerged?
- What did I need then that I did not receive?
- Can I give or extend that unmet need to myself now?
- What capacities do I have to meet and address the concerns my anxiety is trying to protect me from?

Through this exercise, you might make connections you had not previously recognized. You may also recognize that your anxiety, even when it is causing you pain, is trying to help or protect you. Seeing your anxiety in this way invites compassion for yourself and for your anxiety

These questions may also help you to identify more constructive ways of meeting the need seeking to be expressed through your anxiety, as well as your own capacities to handle what is in front of you. Seek to connect yourself to what is true in the present moment and anchor yourself in whatever strengths, resources, and abilities you possess that will help you should the need arise. Recognize the inner calm, strong, resilient parts of yourself that have handled problems in the past and can do so now. With this reframe, you can invite your anxiety to step back, reassuring it that you hear it, that you are going to be okay, and that you will be able to handle whatever arises.

Acknowledging your anxiety is important because if you ignore your anxious thoughts or actively seek to dismiss them, they may feel the need to ratchet things up to get your attention. Imagine if your house is on fire, and your neighbor sees you sitting calmly in the living room. They may first ring your doorbell. If you don't answer, they may go to the window, jumping up and down and yelling your name to get your attention. If that fails, they may then throw a rock through your window in their desperate attempt to warn you of the danger. This is like what anxiety does if you simply try to ignore it without acknowledging it. It will amplify the ways it seeks to get your attention. You can acknowledge the anxiety and the good that it is trying to do, without attaching to its fear-based stories.

Envisioning a persona, character or physical manifestation of your anxiety may help you to detach from it and communicate with it in a more constructive way. Once you see it as something separate from you – not you – new ways of relating to it and being in relationship with it more easily emerge. Just as was true for Robert, the more you see your anxiety as something trying to help you, the more compassion you can develop for it. And this compassion can unlock new ways of interacting with your anxiety that eases it.

Too, when you identify the younger versions of yourself your anxiety is seeking to protect, you can also more easily identify the wound or hurt it is guarding.

This recognition and insight will then help you to consider what the young, hurt version of you needed then, so that you can provide that for yourself now. Once Kelly understood what her anxiety was seeking to protect her from, she was able to provide meaningful reassurance to 5-year-old Kelly, who felt so embarrassed and inadequate, that she had nothing to fear because she was capable of overcoming her early challenges – not by pushing herself through self-criticism, but because of her innate abilities. When Kelly's familiar anxiety emerged, she saw it as a cue to connect to her young self who felt exposed and inadequate, and to speak to it now in the way she wished an adult had spoken to her then. Each time she practiced this, she felt the anxiety release its grip, and she found herself more easily able to move through it, while gradually becoming more accepting of her capabilities and accomplishments.

Chapter 14

Case Study: Hailey

Hailey had a complex history related to her mental health. She had experienced significant trauma, both as a child and a young adult. She struggled with a myriad of mental health symptoms and diagnoses, including anxiety. Hailey had a history of past treatment with therapists, psychiatrists, and inpatient hospitalizations. She was highly dedicated to her health and well-being and worked hard at it. Hailey's anxiety occurred mostly in the form of future catastrophizing, though it also stemmed from distorted beliefs. Due to her trauma history, Hailey was in a near-constant state of hypervigilance and activated anxiety. Her mind was habituated to seeing danger at every turn in the form of catastrophizing, which would then be accompanied by frequent statements of "I can't handle it." This was Hailey's default distorted belief - that she was incapable of handling her emotions or the circumstances of her daily life. Though "I can't handle it" reflected her distorted self-view, it was also a form of catastrophizing in that she was convinced that whatever bad outcomes might happen or feelings she might experience, she would be unable to cope.

When Hailey began therapy with me, she was taking several prescribed psychotropic medications which were essential to her stability and well-being. This included multiple daily doses of Xanax, prescribed by her psychiatrist, to help manage her acute anxiety.

I worked with Hailey on her catastrophizing by naming it each time it presented itself in our sessions. After calling out the catastrophizing, I worked with Hailey to identify what she knew to be true and what stories she was making up. I engaged Hailey in reality testing her fears. Did the things she worried about actually happen? How did she feel on the other side of the situation when her fear failed to materialize? How did she feel on the other side of the situation when some aspect of her fear happened? How did she handle it?

Simultaneously, Hailey and I explored her trauma history. We identified how she learned at a young age to cope with the trauma and what behaviors she adopted because of it. While honoring how these behaviors served a useful purpose for her at one time in her life, we worked to release these behaviors as they were no longer helping and were in fact hurting her.

One adaptive response no longer serving her was disconnection from her feelings and sense of identity. Dissociating from her feelings was protective and necessary when Hailey was living in her childhood home where she felt genuinely unsafe and unprotected. Had she been connected to her experiences and feelings at that time it would have overwhelmed her ability to cope, so she took care of herself by disconnecting from them. What this looked like in her adult life was not being attuned to her genuine feelings and needs and overly deferring to others. I worked with Hailey to become attuned to her feelings, wants, and needs, and to develop healthy and adaptive ways of expressing them.

One example of this was her intense discomfort when going home to visit her family because of how unsafe she felt around her childhood abuser. Despite knowing that she felt intensely anxious and uncomfortable, and that the consequences of these feelings impacted her for days or weeks after a visit, Hailey never allowed for the possibility of setting up her visits home to accommodate her feelings. Hailey worried her mother would be disappointed by, or unsupportive of her doing so. This fear stopped her from attending to her own needs.

I worked with Hailey on identifying what she would want to do to better attend to her feelings and needs – which was to stay at a hotel – and then to consider doing so. This was accompanied by intense anxiety on Hailey's part, including catastrophizing about what would happen if she set this boundary. It was a milestone in therapy for Hailey when she made her first visit home and stayed at a hotel. Her mother was disappointed but accepted it. Hailey felt much better having a safe and neutral space to retreat to when needed. The visit had less emotional wear and tear on her and her relationship with her spouse. And all the catastrophizing that she had imagined about what it would mean to stay at a hotel never materialized. Hailey, from that point on, stayed at hotels, without question or struggle, on every subsequent visit.

After some time in therapy, Hailey would often start a session by saying, "I was catastrophizing," and then would proceed to tell me about moments of anxiety from the week she recognized as being fueled by catastrophizing. In some instances, she was able to stop the anxiety through this awareness. She would engage the questions she had learned to ask to differentiate between *what is* and *what if*. She would use the many tools and techniques she learned in therapy to disengage from the story, calm her anxiety, refocus her thoughts, and reassure herself through mantras that were both soothing and true.

We also worked on Hailey's self-concept and her often repeated refrain, "I can't handle it." Part of this work included reality testing, challenging and reframing this belief. It involved understanding the purpose of this self-belief and opening space for a new self-concept. We talked about "I can't handle it" as both a distorted belief and a form of catastrophizing. The truth was that despite significant anxiety, depression and other challenging symptoms, Hailey did "handle it". She graduated from college and graduate school, was successful in her career, had close and supportive relationships, and hobbies she was skilled in and derived pleasure from. Over time, Hailey began to shift the way she saw herself. She changed "I can't handle it" to "I am strong, capable, loved". She later got a tattoo of those words - *strong, capable, loved*- written in her own handwriting, which I think is beautiful.

Our work together ended when Hailey moved to another state. When she left, she set a goal to wean herself off her daily doses of Xanax under the support and supervision of her psychiatrist and new therapist. Over the years, Hailey sent me occasional life updates. In one, Hailey shared that she had successfully weaned off all Xanax, an incredible testament to her hard work and progress over her anxiety. In another update, Hailey shared that she and her partner were hopefully pregnant. She wrote that they had a positive pregnancy test and an initial ultrasound showing signs of pregnancy. The following week they had a second ultrasound which introduced some uncertainty about the viability of the pregnancy. She wrote, "I am trying to hold on to what we know. The sac is measuring the right size. There is a yolk sac. We may have seen a heartbeat. We will know more on Wednesday. A nice skill you taught me!! Focus on what I know."

I was thrilled to know that years after our work together ended, Hailey was still able to control her catastrophizing.

Chapter 15

Review of Key Strategies for Catastrophizing

1. Differentiate between the facts you know and the story you are telling yourself. Then, focus only on the facts.

- What am I afraid of?
- Of the things I am afraid of, what do I know to be factually true at this moment?
- Of the things I am afraid of, what is the story I am creating?
- When I focus only on the facts, how do I feel?
- When I focus only on the facts, what do I want to do?

2. Mindfulness

- Observe your thoughts and feelings from a detached and non-judgmental stance.
- Think of your thoughts and feelings as clouds passing by or leaves floating down a stream.
- Focus on your breath as a way to detach from thoughts and feelings.

- Use movement if a quiet mindfulness practice is uncomfortable
- Bring your attention and focus to the here-and-now moment
- Practice Wise Mind

3. Grounding

- Place your feet on the floor and look around you, taking in as many details as possible.
- Use all of your senses to be fully present in the moment.

4. Collecting Positives and Gratitude.

- Keep a list or journal of positive experiences and interactions.
- Keep a gratitude journal
- Write thank you letters
- Collect moments of gratitude in a gratitude jar

5. Becoming comfortable with uncertainty

- Reframe uncertainty from fear to possibility.
- Ask yourself: What good things might happen?
- Accept that you cannot (and do not need to) know the unknowable.

6. Befriending your anxiety

- How might your anxiety be trying to help you?

- How is it seeking to protect you?
- Let your anxiety know that you hear it.
- Thank it for trying to protect you.
- Reassure your anxiety that it can step back and that you can handle things from here.
- Create a personification or image of your anxiety to externalize it.

The Antidotes
to Control

Chapter 16

Trust Thyself

Anxiety arising from the need for control has two main characteristics. First, it involves an intense focus on what lies beyond your control, often accompanied by a tendency to overlook what is within your control. The second characteristic involves an ingrained, often subconscious default belief, "I am not okay" or "It will not be okay." These silent convictions have a powerful impact on how you perceive and react to the world as you seek a feeling of safety and security.

The traits of anxiety stemming from control are:

- Rigid behaviors and beliefs about the right way to do things or how you want things to be done
- Strong opinions/beliefs about what others should or should not do or a strong focus on the behavior and choices of others
- Difficulty relaxing because of all the things that need to be done before you can rest
- Feeling overly responsible for others
- Over-preparing

- Over-researching
- Difficulty making decisions
- Perfectionism
- Anticipating and making plans for all that could go wrong (and feeling exhausted from doing so)

At its core, this anxiety stems from a lack of trust in your safety and security. Instead of recognizing that you already possess all that is needed to navigate difficulties, you rely on external factors - such as high standards, rigid expectations and meticulous preparation - as the foundation for feeling secure. The underlying fear is that something will go wrong, and it or you will not be okay. You then rely on over-functioning and over- preparing behaviors, and self-imposed perfectionism and rigidity about how things need to be done as the basis for trusting that you and "it" will be okay. The behaviors stemming from anxiety rooted in control are all attempts to feel comfortable and secure. The problem is they ultimately do not work and cause significant stress.

Those whose anxiety originates from a need for control often express feelings of not just anxiety, but also stress, exhaustion and overwhelm – more so than those whose anxiety is rooted in catastrophizing or distorted beliefs.

The antidotes to anxiety stemming from control focus on cultivating an internal sense of trust that no matter what happens, you are the reason you will be okay. It also involves refocusing your attention from what is not in your control to what is. And finally, learning to do less and to let go; recognizing that attempts to control your environment are doomed to fail, unsustainable and exhausting – and ultimately unnecessary.

Chapter 17

Cultivating an Internal Sense of Trust

Jackie began therapy with me for anger issues. She was increasingly irritable and reported feeling angry "all the time", especially towards her boss. Jackie was an associate professor in philosophy, working towards tenure. She objectively had many demands and expectations to meet, and her ability to achieve tenure was dependent on her success in meeting these demands.

One day, Jackie began her session agitated and clearly frustrated. "I had a really bad week. I'm so angry at my department chair. He called me into his office and gave me a brand-new task to do. I don't know how he expects me to do one more thing on top of everything else he has given me! It's completely unreasonable and I'm really struggling to control my anger around him. I'm afraid I'm going to blow up at him."

I asked Jackie to tell me everything she had to do and what things were expected of her. The list was long. It was legitimately a lot. One of her responsibilities was to teach undergraduate classes three days/week. I asked Jackie how long she spent preparing for each class.

She responded, "4 hours".

That sounded like a long time to me.

"Are these classes that you've taught before?" I asked.

"Yes."

"Are the classes in a subject area you feel comfortable with?"

"Yes, it's what I did my dissertation on."

"What are your student evaluations like?"

She smiled. "They're always great. It's probably one of my biggest strengths."

"Jackie, I don't think you need to spend four hours preparing for each class."

When I said this, she protested. Jackie appeared tense and uncomfortable, clearly not believing my assessment of the situation. She argued that the reason she had such good evaluations from her students was because of the time and thought she put into preparing. This is typical of the objection raised when control is challenged. Jackie believed her anxious behaviors, in this case, over-preparing, were the reasons she was successful.

I said, "I promise you the reason you are successful is not the four hours you put into preparing for the class. It's you. It's your knowledge, your expertise in the material, and your teaching style that are the reasons you are successful. These are all things that are in you and part of you; you do not have to prepare for them to show up."

She sat silently, considering this, and then nodded. I asked if she was willing to work towards reducing the amount of time she spent preparing. She was, and we made a plan for her to reduce her preparation time by 30 minutes per class. I intended to go slow, gradually reducing her prep time to perhaps a quarter of what she was currently doing.

My next appointment with Jackie was two weeks later. She was noticeably more relaxed and excitedly announced that she had reduced her preparation time from four hours to 30 minutes or less. She had even taught some classes with no prep time at all. Jackie had taken her homework and ran with it! I was impressed by her ability to so easily internalize this concept and to trust herself enough to let go as much as she did.

"Tell me, how did it feel going into the classes with so much less preparation?"

"I'm not going to lie. In the first class or two, I was very nervous. I was sure I wouldn't know what to say or how to pace the class. But once I started teaching, it all flowed, and it felt good. Truthfully, I think the classes went just as well as when I spent a lot more time preparing for them."

At the end of the semester, her evaluations were as good as they had always been. She never returned to over-preparing for teaching, having proven to herself it was not necessary. Having let go of this excessive self-imposed expectation, she felt more relaxed and less overwhelmed and angry. This contributed to her growing confidence in her ability to successfully manage the many tasks required of her to achieve tenure.

The behaviors associated with anxiety rooted in control can be categorized as seeking to control one's external environment and anticipating and planning for everything that can go wrong.

While control may give you a sense of security and stability in the short term, it is ultimately unsustainable and leads only to anxiety and stress. Trying to control your external environment is destined to fail because there will always be things outside of your control. I would argue there will often be more things outside your control than within it. On the other hand, trust allows you to let go of the need for control and instead focus on your inner strength and resilience. Placing your trust in yourself can lead to a greater sense of peace and fulfillment. The release that comes with letting go can yield possibilities, opportunities, and feelings of ease and enjoyment that may be inaccessible

to you when your attention is focused outward –
beyond yourself and where you have no control.

Anticipating and planning for what will go wrong is
also ineffective because you cannot know what will
happen in the future. None of us are fortune tellers -
clairvoyance is not a reliable human trait. When
problems arise and things go wrong, as they inevitably
will, you will need to respond based on the information
available to you at that time. You will never be able to
foresee or predict those details. Your ability to manage
the things that go wrong will not depend on your pre-
determined plans. It will depend upon you and all the
internal and external resources you possess.

When I talk about internal resources, I am referring
to the qualities, abilities, and skills you possess. The
aspects of you that remain constant, no matter what
challenges or crises you face. They include your
intelligence, problem-solving skills, creativity,
resourcefulness, analytical abilities, knowledge, and
experience. External resources refer to your support
network, others who possess an expertise or skill set
that you lack, money, and sources of information.

To alleviate anxiety that arises from a need for
control, the goal is to transfer your sense of well-being
from factors outside of yourself to internal ones. It is to
cultivate a sense of trust that you will ultimately be
alright because you, and all your resources, can be
relied on to manage and cope with whatever situation
you face.

151

To help you begin this work of internalizing your sense of trust, make a list of your internal and external resources. Some questions to help you generate this list are:

- What things am I good at that come easily or naturally to me?
- What qualities do I bring to any situation or setting I am in?
- What traits do I possess that are repeatedly recognized or affirmed across jobs or settings, particularly those that feel effortless?
- What skills have I acquired in my career?
- What skills do I possess outside of work?
- What traits or attributes would I be unable to change, no matter how hard I tried?
- When I need help or support, who are the people I can reach out to?
- If I have a problem to solve or a question, to whom or what can I turn for help or answers?
- What assets do I possess that could assist me if I were in a crisis?

Next, think about the tasks and responsibilities that are the source of the most stress in your life. Are there things that keep you awake at night because you cannot stop worrying about them? What tasks do you mentally think about the most? Write these things down.

As you consider the stressful tasks on your list, reflect on the following questions.

- Are there any internal or external resources I identified that I could lean into and trust to show up for me without effort or worry?
- Are there any skills, knowledge, personality traits, or capabilities I recognize in myself that contribute to my success?
- Around persistent worries I carry, what does my history and experience around those worries tell me that I might be able to lean into with greater self-trust? For instance, are there things I routinely worry about, yet my experience with them is consistently one of success or competency?

The reason my intervention with Jackie worked was her openness to considering that it was her own knowledge, skill and capabilities that were behind her success as a teacher, not her preparation time. I have shared this story with many clients, nearly all of whom initially objected that it would be impossible for them, and the requirements of their profession, to similarly reduce the demands they place on themselves. This includes a high-power attorney litigating multimillion-dollar lawsuits, a college professor, and a high-producing sales executive.

There are, of course, many things you need to prepare for. I am not advocating for adopting a stance that everything will be okay no matter what you do or don't do. For anyone whose anxiety stems from a need for control, it would be impossible to simply not care and throw all caution to the wind. However, for each of the clients listed above, when they worked on internalizing their sense of trust and leaning into their talents, strengths, skills, and attributes – the ones that always exist – they were able to let go significantly of the time they felt compelled to spend on some work-related tasks. After succeeding in doing so, none wished, or felt it necessary, to return to their former practices of over-preparing.

In all my years of practice, not once have I seen this result in less success or recognition.

To be clear, it is not that they stopped preparing for their responsibilities or became lackadaisical about their work. They became better at discerning which efforts were necessary and which ones were ineffective. Universally, those who have been able to shift their trust to internal factors have all reported being happier, more relaxed, less anxious, and equally successful.

At times, I struggle with my own version of this. Another type of work I do in my practice is completing clinical assessments and evaluations for clients of immigration lawyers. This involves conducting an extended interview and then writing a clinical assessment in the form of a legal affidavit. Often, there is a deadline associated with these reports, some are firm and dictated by the court system, and others are self-imposed.

I often notice myself feeling stressed about writing the report after I have conducted an interview. I am constantly aware of the need to write the report, sometimes with a sense of worry about how I will fit it into my already busy schedule. When this stress feels unnecessarily high, I stop and ask myself, "Have I ever missed a deadline or been unable to complete a report by the date it was due?" The answer is no. I then remind myself that given my history, there is no reason for me to worry that I won't get this report done. This helps me to detach from unnecessarily worrying about, and mentally reminding myself, that I need to write the report. I can trust myself that I am aware of needing to write the report, and it will get done on time – without my stressing about it to make it so.

Chapter 18

Good Enough: Letting Go of Perfectionism

For many people who experience anxiety from control, they hold themselves to very high standards. They are often perfectionists, fearing that if their actions are not perfect, they are not good at all. I would be hard pressed to think of any instance where something must be done perfectly to be good or of value. This is a false construct. It is unattainable and exhausting. For many, it is accompanied by feelings of anxiety - a fear that if not done perfectly, something bad will happen, something will go wrong, or it will not be okay.

The antidote to perfection is good enough. When I talk about the concept of good enough with clients, it is often met with resistance. It is heard as having no standards and not caring at all about how something is done. It is perceived to mean having no pride in the quality of one's efforts. What good enough actually refers to is the point at which additional effort will not yield an equivalent improvement in the quality of what

157

is produced. I think of this in terms of the law of diminishing returns. The extra effort, stress, and work you expend will come at a cost without any corollary gain in the value of your product.

For Jackie, the point of good enough for preparing for her classes was 30 minutes or less, not the four hours she initially put in. Those extra 3 ½ hours spent preparing did not yield any better results than 30 minutes. But the cost of those extra 3 ½ hours was significant.

The concept of good enough can apply to many moments and aspects of your life. It may refer to your house being clean enough so that you can relax and spend time doing things that will replenish or refresh you. It may be the amount of time you spend working on a job-related task before determining that it is complete. It may be a relaxation of your standards for the kind of meal you feel compelled to prepare when you are hosting family or friends. Or perhaps how much research you do before deciding about a purchase or making a plan.

Josh came to therapy identifying that he was stressed, unhappy, exhausted, and irritable. He often reported feeling "worn down" and found nearly all aspects of his life to be hard. Behind these feelings was anxiety stemming from control. Josh had high standards for himself and took pride in all that he did. For example, when inviting friends over for dinner, it was always an elaborate dinner party including great attention to details such as the flower arrangements he composed himself, and the elaborate way he decorated and set the table. The food itself was all high end and prepared from scratch. His standards meant that his home was beautifully decorated and always clean. While he enjoyed hosting people, he routinely found that by the time his guests arrived, he was exhausted and did not feel as relaxed and present as he would like.

Josh had the same approach when he planned a trip, spending hours reviewing accommodation options. Before he made a purchase, he did extensive research on consumer reviews. He would sit down to do a "little research," and next thing he knew, hours had passed, and he felt no closer to making a decision than before he began.

Was he rewarded in his personal and professional life for holding these high standards and attention to detail? Absolutely! And it all came at a price. Josh was highly stressed and chronically unhappy. He experienced little joy or even contentment in his life.

As is often true with all manifestations of anxiety stemming from control, Josh's high standards were driven by a fear that if he relaxed these standards in any way, his life would not work properly. He attributed his success to his high standards. What I knew to be true for Josh was that if he could relax his standards, he would be just as successful and accomplished, and he would be more at ease and happier.

159

In one session, Josh expressed how stressed he was about planning a family vacation. He elaborated by describing his search for the "perfect" vacation rental for his family. He had spent hours looking at options, reading reviews, poring over pictures, and was unable to make a decision. His indecisiveness was based on his almost obsessive pursuit of the "right" choice, which implied that there was one "right" choice and all others would be "wrong."

"Josh, what do you fear will happen if you stop researching and make a decision?"

"That something won't be right about the decision I make, and it will ruin the trip. I want to make sure we stay somewhere safe. Also, someplace that will be easy to navigate with a stroller. And that's child friendly. I don't want to worry about my daughter breaking things."

"I know how detail oriented you are. I can only assume that when you're reading reviews and looking at photos, you're doing so with those needs in mind."

"Yes, I am."

"What have you experienced that makes you so worried about this? That you might make a decision that will ruin the trip?"

"What do you mean?"

"What are the bad experiences you have had, traveling or otherwise, that have you so worried about your ability to make a good choice now?"

There was silence as Josh considered this. He then said, "Nothing that I can think of. But I think that is because I am so careful and make sure that I don't make mistakes."

"Yours is one way to approach making decisions, and I know you are very effective. And it is not the only way. You have described your husband as much more relaxed and seemingly unconcerned with the details you consider to be important."

"Definitely!"

"When you look at his decision making, what bad decisions and problems has he created through his approach?"

"What do you mean?"

"Well, since we are talking about planning trips, what travel disasters have occurred due to his inattention to detail?"

"Nothing I can think of."

"Okay, so that tells you that one can approach planning for a trip in a different way and do so without any major problems or disasters."

Josh fidgeted in his chair, seemingly uncomfortable as he said, "Yes, but I could never wing it as much as he does."

"I understand that. And I am not asking you to. I just want you to notice that his approach, while very different from yours, works."

He shrugged. "I guess."

"Is that not true? What did I not get right?"

"No, it is true."

"Josh, you are thoughtful, detail oriented, and attuned to the needs of your family. You do not wing it, as you said. You think things through, you do research, and you make informed decisions. I want you to trust that. I want you to know that this is always true and is something you do not need to work at to be true. It is how you approach all decisions."

Josh was silent, then, unable to argue with this, nodded in agreement."

"And because this is how you approach all decisions; you will make a good choice. Amongst the options you have narrowed it down to, it is unlikely that one is so significantly better than the others to be worth all the time and energy that you are expending on this decision. The price you are paying in stress will not be rewarded with a better outcome. And if you should discover some problem or issue, I have complete confidence in yours and your husband's ability to navigate that."

Josh could recognize intellectually that what I said was true, but he still felt anxious and uncomfortable with the thought of altering his behavior to align with this truth. Remember, between thoughts and feelings, feelings are always more powerful.

I invited Josh to be curious about why he feared letting go of continued research and struggled to trust his ability to make a good (enough) decision, asking him to reflect on when this fear first emerged and why. Josh shared memories of being a young child, perhaps 6 or 7, and his parents frequently fighting in a loud and heated manner which was frightening to him. Often, his father was angry at his mother for her spending habits. His parents divorced when he was 9, and following the divorce, his mother faced constant economic stress and hardships while his father went on to thrive financially. His father would often criticize his mother and blame her for her financial struggles. Josh felt simultaneously sorry for his mother, and responsible for trying to make things easier and better for her. Josh was able to connect with this young, frightened child who internalized a fear of making mistakes because of the fighting and criticism he was exposed to, and who sought to alleviate his mother's stress and to make life easier for her by being "perfect."

Connecting his current feelings and behavior to his attempt to cope with these realities of his upbringing helped him appreciate how he benefited from this coping strategy. Acknowledging the toll that it was now taking on his life opened up space within Josh to willingly try new approaches.

I asked Josh to close his eyes and to sit in this truthful version of himself; he is thoughtful, detail oriented, attuned to the needs of his family, and able to identify numerous options that will work well. I asked him to allow for the possibility of trusting these truths about himself. I then asked Josh what he would do if he could approach choosing lodging for his family from this place of trust.

"I would know that I have researched enough, and I would allow myself to make a decision and move on."

"Yes! And how do you imagine it might feel, if you were able to do that?"

"Freeing", he said with an exhale and a relaxing of his shoulders. "Relieving. I would be much less stressed. Planning the trip would probably feel more fun for me and my husband."

"I think you are right. Let's see if we can help move you towards that."

I then worked with Josh to create a plan for making a decision that would limit further research and indecisiveness. He agreed to select two options from those he had already narrowed down to share with his husband for his input. We discussed setting a timer to limit the amount of time allowed for him to review the choices he had bookmarked. If his husband had no input or felt they were both good choices, he agreed to make a reservation, again limiting the amount of time that he was allowed to reflect and decide further.

We anticipated he would feel anxious and that his anxiety would try to convince him that he could make a "wrong choice" and that something bad was going to happen. He prepared himself for this by being ready to thank his anxiety for looking out for him and for trying to keep him and his family safe. He would affirm, out loud, if necessary, his thoroughness and ability to make good decisions, and that no matter what happened, he and his husband would be able to handle it.

Josh did make a reservation at a rental home the next day. Whenever his anxiety tried to second guess the decision or goad him into rethinking it, he provided reassurance to himself that he had given it ample thought and research and that the choice he made was a good enough one. Josh was able to experience some relief after having made the decision. He found that making a decision felt better than continuing to pursue the "right" or "perfect" decision. Though not easy, Josh reported that being able to trust himself and let go ultimately felt much better than the need to keep questioning and researching. The more Josh practiced this with other decisions, the better he got at it.

Now it's your turn. Let's create an experiment for you.

1. Identify an area or areas in your life in which you would like to reduce your stress or anxiety.
2. Next, create an experiment that reduces the amount of time you spend on the identified task(s), just as Jackie did with preparation for teaching or Josh did with researching hotels. For instance, if your goal is to dedicate more time to your family upon returning from work, you might try setting boundaries by designating specific periods during which work is off-limits and refrain from using your phone or other electronic devices during these times.
3. Start reducing your time or energy by small amounts and notice if there is any change in the quality of the outcome.
4. If possible, pair this reduction in work or stressful activities with an increase in a desired and enjoyable activity. As you experiment with these shifts in your behavior, pay attention to the experience.
   - How does it feel?
   - Did it create any negative consequences or negatively impact your effectiveness?
   - What objective feedback did you receive - good or bad - about the quality of your reduced efforts?

- Did it yield any positive feelings or outcomes?

While you seek to reduce "unnecessary" work (physical and mental), your anxiety will sound the alarm that something terrible will happen because you are relaxing expectations and demands of yourself. It will seek to convince you that you will miss the deadline, you will do poorly on an important task, or you will fall short in some important way. The objection used by control is an insistence that it is your anxiety behaviors that are the reason you are successful.

Reflect on when the anxiety beneath this belief began. Just as I asked Josh to consider when his anxious pursuit of perfection began and why, ask yourself what you fear, when you first felt that fear, and what contributed to that fear.

- How might the fear be an attempt at keeping you safe?
- What does your fear want you to know?
- What do you want your fear to know?

Beyond connecting with the origin of your anxiety and how it is seeking to protect you, using the strategies to ease anxiety discussed in Chapter 2 will be useful. You must tolerate the discomfort of trying something new and unfamiliar. The following strategies will help you:

167

- Identify your discomfort as anxiety.
- Start small, with low-stakes tasks.
- Identify and write down your strengths, innate characteristics, and past track record as a reminder that you possess competencies you can trust.
- If there is a brief, affirmative, and true statement that captures this, writing it down as a visual reminder can be helpful. Examples might include:
  - "I have a track record of being competent at X, which I can trust is part of me always."
  - "I am capable and successful, even when things are hard."
  - "I have met and managed every challenge that has come my way, and I can trust that I will continue to do so."

Finding the threshold of good enough will be unique to each person. Remember, good enough is the point at which you will achieve the desired outcome and beyond which any additional effort will not yield better results. It is also the point at which something can be imperfect, yet truly good. Finding your line of "good enough" is a process and may take some experimentation. Be patient and kind to yourself if it takes time to find this balance.

Chapter 19

How to Do Less

You may notice by now a pattern in those whose anxiety stems from control. They are high-functioning, effective, successful, competent and highly stressed individuals. They are over-functioners with high standards and expectations. They have a never ending to do list, and struggle to relax if any item is incomplete. And they will often argue for the necessity of this. If they don't do it, who will? Or, if they don't do it now, it will just pile up, leaving more to do later and more cumulative stress. Tied up in all of this is a visceral discomfort, if not fear, that if they relax and don't keep *doing,* things will fall apart, something bad will happen, or their life will not work properly. It is difficult to feel contentment, happiness, or even joy when consumed by a never-ending to-do list that takes precedence over relaxation, rest, and fun.

The solution is to become comfortable doing less.

I understand that if you are someone who struggles with this form of anxiety, this solution may feel impossible and perhaps unwanted. You may think of all the reasons why this is not possible for you, running through all your essential daily responsibilities that won't get done if you don't do them.

I honor this and do not wish to diminish or invalidate these things nor negate the possibility that you would benefit from more help from people around you. And I want you to understand these thoughts are, in part, the objection raised by control when it is challenged. Your anxiety will seek to convince you that you must continue to function as you are for your life to work and for you to be okay. However, there is a way in which you can learn to do less, for the reward of less anxiety, increased feelings of ease, and greater enjoyment of your life.

If you have identified that your anxiety is based in control, then you are a highly capable and competent person. And I promise you can lose your anxiety and keep all your competence.

On one of my favorite podcasts, a popular psychologist described a dynamic with her husband at home in which she was constantly aware of all the things that needed to be done before she could allow herself to relax. She would see the dishes in the sink and the laundry that needed to be folded and put away and would feel the need to take care of it all before resting. She could connect this behavior to the messages she internalized in her family of origin that placed a moral value on doing as much as one can at all times.

Her husband, not socialized in the same way in his own family, was able to relax and sit on the couch in the middle of the day. This frequently irritated her. However, she recognized that her need to be busy was unhealthy and caused her undue stress and anxiety. One day, she went to her husband and said, "I need your help learning how to sit on the couch."

She described feeling intensely vulnerable and uncomfortable saying this to him. Doing so reflected her ability to reframe his sitting on the couch as a strength that represented his ability to honor rest and relaxation. She recognized it is important to be able to pause in the middle of the day to rest, or to allow for more fun. Learning to do so was not easy, and initially uncomfortable. She also found that the house did not fall apart. The laundry still got put away, the dishes still got washed, and the family still got fed. Over time, she learned to do less and felt more fully human as a result.

This concept of over-functioning may exist within relationship dynamics that need to recalibrate the balance of who does what. I am intentionally naming this, and choosing to not address it, as this is a topic for a different book altogether (and there are several excellent ones already written such as *Fair Play* by Eve Rodsky and *Equal Partners* by Kate Mangino). Yet, I invite you to consider what you would like to do less of. Or what things would you like to do more of but feel unable to because of your to-do list? In addition to the validity of your to-do list, is it possible that your difficulty letting go of what gets done and how it gets done is contributing to your feelings of stress? Might you be complicit in your own oppression?

As I focus on the global concept of cultivating an internalized sense of trust, if you are a person who is trapped in a state of over functioning, you may argue that the problem is not that you don't trust yourself; it is that you don't trust others to do things as well as you would do them. You may argue that you trust yourself too much. And while this is unquestionably true, what also goes hand in hand with this is the belief that if you don't do it or if it's not done the way you would do it, then it won't be okay. This is another form of not trusting – not trusting that if you are not the one in control, things can still be okay. This is a belief that needs to be challenged.

When I pointed out to Josh that his husband, who approaches things in a different way than he, has never experienced any disasters when planning for trips, I was seeking to illuminate that there is more than one way to do things, all of which can lead to the same outcome. This is a universal truth. Your path may be highly effective. It is unquestionably one that makes you feel comfortable and safe. And yet there are other paths that will also lead to the desired outcome.

When you consider doing less, you will inevitably need to let go of some tasks and responsibilities. And you will also have to let go of how they get done. This will likely feel uncomfortable. One strategy that can help with this is to discuss what the desired and mutually agreed upon outcome is with the person(s) whose cooperation, help or support you will need. When there is agreement, your job is then to let go of the process of how it gets done. For instance, if you and your spouse agree that they will prepare lunches for your children, you must refrain from directing what and how they pack—trusting their ability as a co-parent. I would encourage you to remove yourself as fully as possible to avoid any temptation to control how the task gets completed.

Here are some questions for you to reflect on to help you identify ways to do less.

- Are there tasks or activities that I do out of guilt or because I feel obligated?
- Are there tasks that I do because I don't want to disappoint someone?
- If I felt able to say no, what things would I take off my plate?
- Are there things I do because I am afraid of a bad outcome if I were to stop?

Write down in one column all the things you identify that you don't want to be doing, or that you want to do less of. In a column next to this, write down what you would have to let go of to stop doing these things. By this I mean what things you would have to be willing to tolerate to give yourself permission to do less.

- Would I have to let go of worrying about what someone else thinks?
- Would I have to tolerate possibly disappointing someone?
- Would I have to let go of how the task or activity gets done if I wasn't the one doing it?
- Would I have to tolerate the possibility that it won't get done at all?

In a final column, write down what you might gain if you let go of these tasks, or did less. You may have to imagine a future version of yourself who has succeeded in letting go. What might you gain?

- More time?
- Less stress?
- Engaging in activities that feel more meaningful?
- More fun and joy?
- Feeling more fully human?

Once you have identified some tasks that you would like to let go of, I invite you to consider an experiment for yourself to do just that. I am calling it an experiment because it is something you can play with to see what happens. It is not something you need to commit to long term.

In thinking about constructing an experiment for yourself, consider who you may need support from to put this plan into action.

Hilary decided once she was an empty nester, she did not want to make dinner every night. She had a conversation with her husband communicating this wish, and he agreed to make dinner on certain nights each week. For both, the process of letting go was not always easy and required adjustments on both sides. For Hilary, she found that to resist stepping in to advise or "help", she had to stay away from the kitchen when he was preparing the meal. Likewise, he tended to ask for help more than was needed when Hilary was present. By removing herself he was less inclined to ask for help.

They had to negotiate through positive and constructive communication. Hilary needed him to truly own the task, meaning that he figured out the answers to his questions without her. If he was making a recipe, he was responsible for making sure he had all the necessary ingredients. If he did not know where something was, he was to look for it before asking her where to find it. If he had a question about measurements, cooking time, substitutions, etc. he had to look it up rather than ask her. What he needed from her was permission to prepare the meal in his own way without critique if he did things differently than how she would have done it.

Through trial and error, and ongoing communication, they succeeded in shifting dinner to a more shared responsibility. Over time, this became a routine free from the tension and conflict experienced early in the process. At times, they reverted back to old, familiar patterns, but having succeeded in establishing new behaviors, they were able to correct this with relative ease. Upon recognizing her success in letting go of this task, Hilary identified other places in her life where she could further let go of tasks and responsibilities she no longer wished to claim.

Another practice that many high achievers find helpful when seeking to do less is to schedule time into their day or week for fun, rest or "doing nothing". I view this as a steppingstone to creating more balance in your life. It often feels like a bridge too far to honor rest, relaxation and fun. Just as the guest on the podcast asked her husband for help sitting on the couch, you may need help in giving yourself permission to do less. Scheduling time for this may provide an access point for you to start.

When engaging in your experiment, anticipate that initially you will feel anxious. You will worry about how things will get done, and what will happen if you are not the one doing them.

Remind yourself of your goal and that this is only an experiment; you are trying this for right now, not forever. Remember that your anxiety will seek to convince you that making changes to how you do things will be met with problems or danger. To help you withstand this objection, remember that there is no such thing as the right way, while everything else is the wrong way. There are many right ways. Your way is the preferred way, not the only and necessary way.

Notice the outcome each time you engage with the experiment. If it is successful, take this in without discounting it. If it did not work, consider why and if there are any adjustments that need to be made.

One final thing to consider if you are an over-functioner is how being busy to the point of exhaustion might be serving a purpose for you. Is it keeping you from connecting with feelings that might be too painful or overwhelming to feel? Does the busyness serve to keep you from slowing down and having to face aspects of your life or yourself that feel too hard to sit with? If this is the case, you will need to build the capacity to feel your feelings, or to face difficult truths about yourself or your life before you will be able to let go and do less.

The mindfulness and grounding practices discussed in chapters 7 and 8 can be helpful in building your capacity to be with your thoughts and feelings without being overwhelmed by them. Journaling is another useful tool for providing a space to place and process your thoughts and feelings. Writing about your feelings can provide a sense of order and containment for them, to feel less overwhelmed by them. If you are new to journaling, a good place to start is setting a timer for 5 minutes and writing, free association style, whatever thoughts and feelings surface until the timer goes off. Re-reading your journals can expand your ability to be self-reflective, to notice themes and important messages in your thoughts and feelings, to recognize ways in which they shift and change (which can lessen their power) and increase your ability to tolerate them. And therapy can be an essential tool to provide you with a safe space and guide to explore your thoughts and feelings.

Chapter 20

**Letting Go of What
is Not Yours**

Julie was 9 years old when her father died. Her mother
had not worked outside of the home since having
children and was overwhelmed with grief and anxiety
following her husband's death. Julie felt responsible for
making things easier for her mother. She was acutely
aware of all the ways her mother struggled and sought
to ease her mother's burden. She felt responsible for
cleaning the house, cooking and worried about
finances. She tried to anticipate her mother's moods and
needs and sought to be "easy" for her so that Julie was
not an added burden.

Julie carried this overdeveloped sense of
responsibility into adulthood. She anticipated what
others might need or want and tried to problem-solve in
advance for them. When her mother complained to her
about her challenges, Julie offered solutions, which her
mother rarely acted upon. Julie was regularly frustrated
that all her practical solutions to her mother's struggles
were ignored.

Her relationships with her 3 siblings were at times strained, in part because of these behaviors. When they gathered as a family, she tended to over-involve herself in trying to make plans for her siblings in ways beyond anything she was asked to do. Julie then felt angry, frustrated, and resentful when they did not enjoy the activities she planned in the ways she had hoped.

For example, she would stress about choosing a restaurant that everyone would like and make a reservation, all without input, and then when her family just wanted to order pizza, she felt frustrated and unappreciated.

While it was thoughtful of her to anticipate the needs of others when planning family events, she regularly did so without asking them what their concerns were or if they wanted her help. It was true that her mother did regularly vent her anxiety and worries to Julie. And for all the good ideas and solutions Julie offered, she had no power to make her mother act upon any of them.

Attempts to control are often disguised as being helpful or considerate of others. While your actions may appear thoughtful, it's important to recognize the underlying need driving them. Often, the true motivation is to feel comfortable, secure or needed. This is especially true when you take on responsibility for others without being asked or offering help that isn't requested. This isn't to suggest that your intentions aren't good, but rather to acknowledge that, most often, your own comfort is the real driving force—not the other person's. Moreover, when you find yourself strongly invested in someone else's choices and actions, particularly when you are certain you know what is best for them, your energy is directed outside of yourself, onto them - where you have no control. Often what is called for instead is acceptance - acceptance of their choices, wishes, and perhaps their limitations. It does not mean that you approve, like what is happening, or think it is fair or right. Acceptance simply means you acknowledge what you do not have the power to change. This concept sounds simple in theory but is often quite difficult to put into practice.

In Julie's story, her anger, frustration, and resentment were rooted in her tendency to shoulder the burdens of responsibilities that were not truly hers. Her mental and physical energy was consistently invested in matters beyond her control. The journey of our therapeutic work was dedicated to assisting Julie in disentangling herself from these longstanding patterns that dictated her relationships, particularly within her family.

As Julie practiced refocusing her attention on herself, she let go of anticipating her family's needs. What followed was greater ease in her relationships with each family member. She became more open to their ideas and suggestions. She felt less compelled to anticipate and problem-solve, which helped her feel more relaxed. She became more flexible when making family plans, which brought more enjoyment to all of them, including Julie.

Julie worked hard to accept that even though her mother was struggling and venting to Julie about her problems, Julie did not have the power to make her mother act on any of her ideas and solutions. She shifted her focus to listening. If Julie offered suggestions and her mother resisted them, Julie let it go. This led to a closer and more peaceful relationship. Did she continue to worry about her mother and feel frustrated on her behalf? Of course. However, she learned to disengage from feeling responsible for her mother and her choices. She also became more accepting of her mother's way of doing things.

Julie's journey of transformation was aided by cultivating compassion for the roots of her behavior – the profound impact of her father's passing on her and her family. With this self-compassion, she adopted a mantra, telling herself whenever she had the urge to step in to fix, plan or problem solve, "It's not my job, my responsibility, or my problem to fix." Julie honed her ability to discern between what she could and could not control.

In the deliberate practice of building internal trust, especially in moments of anxiety and discomfort, Julie affirmed, "I can let go of worrying about X because it is not in my control and whatever happens, I will figure it out and I will be okay." With each instance of practicing self-trust, Julie witnessed her life flourishing without the weight of trying to single-handedly "hold up the sky" for herself and her family.

If you recognize in yourself a tendency to feel overly responsible for others or things outside of your control, let's help you release this. Take out a piece of paper and write down the people or things for which you have an overdeveloped sense of responsibility. Next, write down your answers to the following questions.

- What experiences or internalized messages from my life contribute to this sense of responsibility?
- What feelings do I associate with my sense of responsibility: Guilt? Obligation? A sincere desire to help others? Where do these feelings come from?
- What am I afraid will happen if I release myself from this feeling of responsibility?
- Of the things I am afraid of, what is in my control?
- Of the things I am afraid of, what is my responsibility versus someone else's responsibility?
- Is it easier for me to focus on others and what they should do than on me and what I might need to do/not do?

Focus your attention on what is within your control and your responsibility. Everything else requires acceptance, recognizing that the actions of others or the outcomes of certain situations are beyond your influence, power, or obligation. Reflecting on the questions above can help you uncover the roots of your heightened sense of responsibility for others and the motivations that keep you tied to this relational pattern.

When embracing acceptance involves recognizing that something problematic, painful or concerning may unfold, give yourself permission to acknowledge your emotions. Feeling sad, frustrated, angry, scared, or disappointed is understandable and appropriate.

If letting go of responsibility means someone you care about may experience an adverse outcome, acknowledge that they have their own agency and ability to make choices. You are not responsible for the decisions and actions of others. Allow them the space to take ownership of their lives – the good, bad, and ugly. Gift them with your trust that they may know better than you what they need or are capable of and your confidence that they can learn and grow from adversity or mistakes. If the choices they make are too painful to witness up close, give yourself permission to take a step back so that you are observing from a more distant vantage point. And above all else, remain grounded in the knowledge that regardless of the outcome, you simply do not have the power to control others.

Avoid the temptation to personalize others choices or abilities and see them as reflections of their care for you. Recognize that a person's actions are almost always a reflection of their abilities, strengths, weaknesses, and circumstances, rather than a reflection of their intentions or feelings towards you. Disengaging from a belief in intention is helpful in achieving acceptance.

When you catch yourself dwelling on or seeking to influence something or someone that is beyond your control, redirect your attention to what is in your control. What is yours to do in this situation?

To help you with this, return to your piece of paper and draw a line down the middle.

- On one side of the line, write down everything that is in your control.
- On the other side, write down everything that is beyond your control.

Your energy and focus will be directed solely towards what you can control. This means making decisions based on what is and how you feel about what is, within your sphere of influence.

Like all other strategies and practices recommended in this book, repetition is required to gain comfort and mastery of the skill. Be gentle with yourself if you find this, or any other skill challenging. Letting go of feeling responsible for others is often complicated by feelings of care for them. Know that you can keep all the care and love you feel, while detaching from the actions that are futile, exhausting, and often harmful to the relationship you care so deeply about.

Chapter 21

Case Study: John

John was a high school science teacher who lived in a state of high anxiety, manifesting as near constant efforts to control his environment. He often felt stressed and irritable, and he was exhausted and depleted by the constant demands for his time and attention. Beyond his responsibilities in the classroom, John would come home from work and immediately attend to household chores. He had a constant to-do list for school running in his mind; prep for future classes, grading, and tasks related to the numerous committees and extracurricular activities he volunteered for. From the time John woke up in the morning until he went to bed, he was in a perpetual state of stress.

John's anxiety was, in part, a coping response to his father's death when John was a child. As the oldest child and only son in the family, John felt responsible for becoming the "man of the house", even though he was only 14 years old at the time of his father's death. His vigilance and high standards around all that needed to be done was rooted in an attempt to create a sense of control and well-being in response to circumstances that left him feeling vulnerable and overwhelmed. This coping mechanism became ingrained in John, and by adulthood, he was convinced it was an intractable character trait.

John sought to protect himself from ever feeling so blindsided and overwhelmed again. He did this by anticipating and planning for catastrophe. John was convinced that doing so gave him an advantageous edge and was the reason he was successful in life. He believed that his "worrying in advance" protected him from bad outcomes.

While I affirmed the seeming logic of this strategy and showed deep compassion for its self-protective nature, I worked with John to understand that his attempts at self-protection were ultimately futile. He would never be able to successfully predict or protect himself from problems, challenges or even tragedies. Instead, he could trust his innate qualities, strengths, and resources to help him to cope with whatever challenges arose.

We worked on all aspects of how control manifested in John's life, including his inability to relax at home. I explored with John what activities would make him feel relaxed and recharged. He expressed the wish to watch a television show with his wife in the evening, to go to the gym a few times a week, and to play his guitar; an activity he enjoyed but rarely made time for. We discussed all the obstacles, which included not being able to relax if there were any dirty dishes in the sink, if laundry was unfolded or not put away, if he had papers to grade or upcoming classes to prepare for. John argued for the need for all this to be done and his inability to relax or enjoy himself if they were hanging over his head. He would say, "I won't be able to relax knowing that there is housework to do or work for school to be done." Or "If I put off doing these tasks, they will just pile up for me to have to do them later."

While acknowledging the importance of his many responsibilities, I affirmed John's skill and competence and introduced the idea that he could do less in all areas causing him stress to make room for himself. I assured John that everything would still get done (though admittedly not necessarily on the same time schedule or in the exact way as before), that he would continue to be successful, and his home and life would not fall apart.

For a long time, John did not buy what I was selling. Each time he rejected this message, I acknowledged where his reluctance stemmed from, framing it as the objection to his anxiety fighting to remain in control. I contextualized his control behaviors as having served him well when he was a child and in life circumstances that were overwhelming and wildly out of his control. I reminded him that he was no longer a child, nor in life circumstances in which he felt so powerless and that his coping methods had served him well and deserved rest after a job well done.

When John was ready to experiment with this idea, we began working to help him to do less. We started small, with the dishes in the sink after dinner. One night, John was particularly tired and wanted to sit on the couch and watch a television show with his wife. There were dishes from dinner still in the sink. John forced himself to leave the dishes and join his wife to watch television. He mentioned the dirty dishes to his wife, who volunteered to do them either that night before bed or in the morning before she went to work. John had to sit with the discomfort of the dishes not getting done when he wanted and potentially not how he wanted. He was able to watch the show and put the dirty dishes out of his mind.

He went to bed that night and left for work the next morning with the dishes still in the sink; something new, unfamiliar, and admittedly uncomfortable for him. When he returned home after work, the dishes were done. John had felt uncomfortable throughout this process but managed this discomfort by consciously tolerating it and managing his response to it.

When I asked John what this had been like for him, he said, "Truthfully, I was uncomfortable, and I was not able to fully relax. But it definitely felt good that I allowed myself to watch the show, and I was proud of myself for leaving for work without doing the dishes. And you were right; the house did not fall down, and the world did not stop because I left dirty dishes in the sink."

John continued to build on this success, finding more things he could let go of to create a greater sense of balance and ease in himself. He learned to postpone certain chores in favor of reading a book or playing guitar.

All the while, he reported that the chores still got done. Gradually, he noticed that he was less preoccupied with what needed to be done in the house and that his mental to-do list had gotten quieter. It was still there; it just wasn't screaming for his attention all the time. And the overall condition and cleanliness of his house did not suffer; how it all got done just looked different and more relaxed.

This carried over into the work he did at home for school. If he had tests to grade but was too tired to do them that night, he would create a plan for when he would get them done and then give himself permission to take the night off. By doing this, he was able to go to the gym 2-3 times a week, read more books, and spend more time connecting with his wife.

John also became more thoughtful and discriminating when it came to extracurricular activities. He gradually let go of commitments he was primarily doing for others or out of an ingrained sense of obligation. He was able to discern between the things that were important and meaningful to him and the things that he did because "no one else would do them" if he did not. Each time he stepped back, someone else stepped in. Often, he stepped out of things not knowing who would step in or how they would get done but was able to recognize that these tasks were not solely his responsibility.

In therapy, John connected with the immense feelings of overwhelm, fear, abandonment and emotional neglect he felt following his father's death. He realized that some of his hyper- functioning was an attempt to avoid his feelings. By allowing himself the space to reflect on and feel his feelings about his father's death, John became less afraid of them. He also came to understand and honor many of his anxiety traits as attempts by his 14-year-old self to take care of him in ways that his devastated mother was unable to do. He recognized that he no longer needed to rely on this hyper-vigilance and attempts to control everything around him. More importantly, he came to understand and eventually believe that doing so was not protecting him in any meaningful way and was causing more stress and harm. This was achieved slowly through repeated practices of letting go and doing less and paying attention to how he felt on the other side of doing so.

Over time, John began to regularly say in session, "I just decided that I was not going to do that. I know it will get done, and everything is going to be fine. And if it's not, I'll figure it out." This is the ultimate statement of an internalized sense of trust. And it is a dramatic shift from how John viewed himself and the world before he began therapy. John still maintains high standards and deeply values his work, home, and relationships. However, as he grew more confident in his abilities and learned to trust himself, he released the stress and control that once dominated his life. He came to understand it as an adaptive response from his younger self, trying to cope with his father's death. With this realization, John was able to let go, do less, and trust more. As a result, he became more relaxed, better able to enjoy life, and more focused on what truly mattered to him, while letting go of what didn't.

Chapter 22

**Review of Key
Strategies for Control**

**1. Cultivate Internalized Trust in Your Well-being and
Competency:**

- Identify your internal strengths and resources that are always present.
- Recognize your external resources, such as people or tools you can rely on when needed.
- Shift your trust from external factors to internal ones, letting go of controlling behaviors that compensate for a lack of trust in yourself and your ability to cope. Honor any past experiences that might have informed your current way of doing things and consider what is different now.

2. Find the Threshold of "Good Enough":

- Acknowledge that perfectionism is unattainable and leads to stress and exhaustion.
- Determine the point at which doing more won't significantly improve results.

195

- Experiment with stopping at the "good enough" point, starting with low-stakes tasks.
- Observe the outcomes of accepting "good enough" and recognize any benefits it brings.

3. Do Less

- Identify obligations you no longer wish to fulfill for others and prioritize your own needs.
- Determine activities or interests you want to dedicate more time to but feel unable to due to external demands.
- Challenge assumptions that certain tasks must be done by you to ensure they are accomplished.
- Conduct personal experiments to create space for your interests by letting go of some tasks and responsibilities.
- Practice positive and constructive communication with people whose help, support or partnership is needed in order to do less.
- Practice saying "no" to requests that you do not want to do.

4. Letting Go of What You're Not Responsible For:

- Differentiate between what you can control and what is beyond your influence.
- When you catch yourself expending excessive energy on uncontrollable factors such as others' thoughts, feelings or actions, redirect your focus

to what you can control: your thoughts and reactions.

- Embrace acceptance, understanding that it doesn't imply approval or agreement, but rather acknowledgment of what you can't change and a desire to seek peace in this.

The Antidotes
to Distorted Beliefs

Chapter 23

The Funhouse
Mirror Analogy

I often describe distorted beliefs through the analogy of looking at oneself through a funhouse mirror. Imagine if this were the only mirror you ever used, and you accepted its reflection as the true image of yourself. You would firmly believe that the too-long arms hanging down below the knees of the too-short legs are an accurate representation of your shape and form. It would alter the way you view yourself, how you feel about yourself, and the way you move through the world.

You may grow to hate or feel disgust with your too long arms or too short legs. You may feel self-conscious about the ways your shape is different from others, and adopt behaviors aimed at hiding or masking these differences. You might avoid activities you are convinced you cannot do because of these flaws. For example, you might become convinced that you cannot run or participate in sports because of your shape and form. You might be reluctant to attend certain social engagements because you do not want to draw attention to yourself or feel uncomfortable interacting with all the "normal bodied" people out there. You would likely feel extremely self-conscious and convinced that your flaws define how others experience and see you. You might decide that people would not want to be your friend or date you because of these flaws.

So, to make yourself worthy of attention, friendship or companionship, you may make yourself excessively accommodating to the needs and wants of others. You convince yourself that this will compensate for the awkwardness of your physical form and give people a reason to want to spend time with you.

Let's take this analogy a step further. Because the mirror you are viewing yourself through is distorted, the way you see yourself is not the way others see you. As you move through the world, you will be told in a variety of ways how you are seen and experienced by others. You may receive compliments about how nice you look in a particular outfit. Or be invited to parties and other social events you feel self-conscious to attend. You may be complimented on your athletic ability. Other talents and qualities you embody might be affirmed across numerous settings, such as in job performance evaluations or in notes of appreciation from friends.

In response to these affirmations, your mind, which is convinced of the validity of the distorted fun house mirror image, will find a way to reject, deflect, minimize, and invalidate each compliment. You will do this by saying, "They are just saying that to be nice," "They don't want to hurt my feelings," "They say that to everyone," "That's easy, anyone could do it," and so on.

If the only mirror you have ever viewed yourself through is a distorted one, you would have no awareness of what is true and what is false. It is you who is not seeing things as they actually are. You are not a reliable witness or narrator.

When anxiety stems from distorted beliefs, not only do you hold negative and false beliefs to be true, but you also have developed maladaptive behaviors that do not serve you. To further complicate matters, distorted beliefs resist change by convincing you that objective evidence—no matter how truthful—is insincere, insignificant, or invalid. This is a lot to sort through. Patience and compassion will be necessary companions on your journey to a healed self-view.

Chapter 24

**Unraveling the False Belief
to Discover What is True**

Let's begin with the distorted belief itself. By definition, this is something you believe to be true, that, in reality, is not. Your negative self-perception likely causes feelings of not only anxiety but depression or sadness as well. For instance, if you believe you are fundamentally flawed, unlovable, inadequate, or lacking some essential quality or skill, it makes sense that you might feel sad, hopeless, defeated, or even self-loathing.

Though you may hold several negatively distorted beliefs, often, these judgments originate from one or two fundamental core beliefs. To help you identify this, take out a piece of paper and write down all the ingrained beliefs about yourself you attach to feelings of sadness or anxiety. Think about situations in which you often or typically feel anxious or depressed and write down the corresponding thoughts and self-beliefs. Are there any recurring themes? Is there one phrase or belief that is repeated often?

Next, on a new piece of paper, write down all the things you do or don't do because of your negative, distorted belief. Be as thorough and exhaustive as you can be. Understanding not only your core negative belief, but also the behaviors you have adopted because of it, is essential to overcoming your anxiety.

One of my core distorted beliefs is that I am or will be awkward. This is a deeply embedded fear/conviction that I can trace back to my very early years. What arose from this belief is shyness and discomfort with drawing attention to myself. Behaviors that stem from this core belief include (but are not limited to) being excessively quiet in classrooms as a young student, not raising my hand in educational settings to ask questions, avoiding activities that draw attention to myself or require an absence of self-consciousness (improv is my personal nightmare!), and avoiding certain unfamiliar social events.

A final piece of reflection I want you to journal about is this: What experiences led you to believe this distorted perception? To help you identify this, think back to your earliest memories associated with this belief or of feeling the emotions attached to it. What was happening? What meaning did you make of it?

Gaining an understanding of the origins of your self-belief is a crucial component in the process of discovering an accurate view of yourself. Distorted beliefs often stem from childhood experiences, including parental influences, responses from primary caregivers or peers, internalized messages expressed directly or indirectly, and the impact of life experiences or environmental realities.

Austrian psychiatrist Rudolf Dreikurs noted that "children are keen observers and poor interpreters". They are keen observers because their minds are like sponges, soaking up details and experiences with great curiosity and openness. However, children are "terrible interpreters" because they lack the necessary knowledge, experience, emotional maturity and cognitive abilities to accurately interpret and make sense of the information they observe. Children may rely on simplistic explanations or make assumptions to fill gaps in their understanding, leading to misconceptions or misunderstandings.

They may generalize based on limited examples or apply rigid thinking patterns that do not account for nuance and complexity. For instance, a sensitive child may grow up believing there is something wrong with them or that they are "too much" based on how their caregivers respond to them if those caregivers fail to understand the deep feeling nature of the child.

This is true for all children. When children experience elements of trauma, parental mis-attunement, or inconsistent and chaotic home environments, their tendency to internalize false beliefs becomes even more pronounced. Children are driven by an innate need to feel safe, protected, and connected. Since children rely entirely on their parents for both their physical and emotional needs, any threat to the parent-child connection can be perceived as a threat to their overall well-being. In such situations, children often unconsciously choose to see themselves as flawed rather than attributing flaws to their parents.

This dynamic serves a dual purpose. Firstly, by internalizing false beliefs, children allow their dependent relationship with their parents to remain intact, preserving the perception that their parents are good and capable. Secondly, it fosters an illusion of control, as children may convince themselves that by taking responsibility and altering their behavior, they can influence outcomes and have their needs met.

My internalized distorted belief of awkwardness did not stem from childhood trauma or a disturbed home environment. It was formed by early childhood experiences in which I felt shy and uncomfortable, over-generalized the experiences, and misinterpreted the source of those feelings. A very early memory that comes to mind- actually two memories - is of being a young child with very short hair. This was in the 1970s when the "Dorothy Hamill" haircut was popular. I had forever tangled hair, and to make brushing it easier, my mother chose to cut my hair in the short and popular style. In addition to my very short hair, I was a girl who hated skirts and dresses. Twice, while quite young, I was with my mother and mistaken for a boy. I have a clear memory of passing a man while walking with my mother who said to her, "That's a nice-looking boy you have." These experiences (and many others), coupled with my innate shyness, contributed to (though in no way was solely responsible for) my discomfort with being noticed and seen and a conviction that I was homely and awkward. This was a belief that I latched onto and struggled to evolve as I evolved.

Lynn grew up as the only child of a single mother who physically took care of her but emotionally was disengaged and attuned only to her own needs and wants. Lynn's emotional needs were never met, because her mother's needs were always first and foremost.

Lynn's survival strategy in this home environment was to pursue perfection. Her hope was that if she met her mother's many needs and was perfectly behaved and accomplished, then she would get some attention and care from her mother. This was not perfectionism driven by the fear that anything less than perfection would be a failure. This was perfectionism rooted in her only perceived hope of getting her needs met.

The failure of this strategy, which was inevitable because the problems and shortcomings resided within her mother and her capacities, not in Lynn, resulted in Lynn concluding that she was unworthy of love. The behaviors that arose from this belief were excessive people pleasing, overextending herself to others in ways that were harmful and hurtful to herself, expecting little from others in relationships, and an inability to set boundaries that reflected how she wanted to be treated by others.

The work of therapy shifted Lynn's view of herself from feeling unworthy of love to feeling worthy and loved. Understanding the source of Lynn's feelings of unworthiness, and the behaviors associated with this belief, were essential ingredients in the recipe for her healing.

After identifying your core distorted belief, a necessary step in the work of overcoming anxiety rooted in distorted beliefs is to identify what is true.

While this may sound simple, it is often not easy. The more attached to the distorted belief you are, the more difficult it will be to consider that something else might be true. A further difficulty is that your distorted belief will fight to preserve itself when challenged by dismissing, deflecting and invalidating objective evidence that tells you the truth.

When considering a replacement belief to work with, whatever you choose must be 100% believable and 100% true to you. You are likely familiar with the concept of positive affirmations - statements or phrases that focus on positive qualities, beliefs, or outcomes. The purpose of positive affirmations is to reframe negative or limiting thoughts and replace them with positive and empowering ones. Affirmations can foster a sense of self-belief and resilience, but they will not work if you do not believe them.

While focusing on and acting from an affirmation you believe to be true and that aligns with your values has been shown to be highly effective in improving mood and self-concept, using affirmations you do not believe are true has been shown to have the opposite effect. Simply choosing the opposite of a negative belief does not necessarily create a useful positive affirmation.

It would not be helpful for me to replace "I am awkward" with an affirmation of "I am never awkward, always perfectly graceful and unconditionally accepted by all". This is not a true or believable statement. What could be helpful to say is, "I am no more awkward than anyone else, and I am generally liked and responded to well by others." If I wanted to simplify it even further, I could say, "We are all awkward sometimes - I, no more so than others." I could borrow the often-repeated phrase used by Brene Brown, the renowned author and researcher on the topic of shame and vulnerability, "Stay kind, brave and awkward" to remind myself that awkwardness is a positive human trait to be embraced. I often focus on a combination of all these thoughts in moments of feeling uncomfortable - reminding myself that to be awkward is to be human, that everyone has awkward moments, and that I can be kind rather than harsh with myself when feeling embarrassment.

It is your turn to work on your corrected belief. On a new piece of paper, write down your primary distorted belief. Then, write down any ideas you have for a new statement that is positive, believable, and true. Look for something that sounds right and feels good to you, but do not be surprised or discouraged if you initially struggle to come up with something.

For Lynn, getting to her corrected belief was a hard-fought battle. Her belief, "I am unworthy of love," was so deeply entrenched that she fought any possible reframing of this with the words, "Yes, but..." She could easily see how others were deserving and worthy of love but could not say that she was. She debated, discounted, and rejected any evidence of her worthiness by countering it with her weaknesses or perceived failures. The care and value shown to her by people in her life was rejected by giving credit to the goodness of the other, not her worthiness.

If you are struggling to find your corrected belief, you can simply identify what you want to be true and then express an openness or willingness to see yourself in that way. For Lynn, this could be to say, "I am willing to see myself as deserving of love." Or "I wish to see myself as worthy of love." What worked for Lynn was, "I give love easily to others and am willing and open to receive love in return."

Once you've identified your corrected belief, practice using it regularly and often. Whenever you catch yourself thinking a distorted thought, replace it with your new belief. Treat it like a mantra, using it to calm the anxiety triggered by the distortion. While this alone won't fully transform your beliefs into more accurate ones, it's an essential part of the process.

Lynn used her corrected belief, "I give love easily and am open and willing to receive love in return," when taking an important step in a one-sided relationship that caused her pain. Past behavior would have had her twisting herself into an "emotional pretzel" to meet this friend's needs and make her happy. Using the mantra to aid her in trying new behavior, Lynn was able to distance herself when her friend made unreasonable demands of Lynn and reacted poorly to Lynn saying no. The mantra helped her to withstand the temptation to smooth things over with her friend by abandoning her no, recognizing that she was being treated in a way that Lynn would not treat someone she cared for. By adjusting her behavior in relationships to reflect her corrected belief, over time, her relationships became more balanced and healthier overall as she shifted her focus to her strong and reciprocal relationships.

Expect that as you practice using your corrected belief, it will feel uncomfortable and unnatural at first. Returning to the funhouse mirror analogy, if the only mirror you ever viewed yourself through was a funhouse mirror, the image in an accurate mirror would look entirely unrecognizable and may feel uncomfortable. Even if the image reflected is more pleasing, you would likely wish to return to the fun house mirror as quickly as possible because it is familiar, comfortable, and therefore safe. However, if you were to challenge yourself to stay in front of the accurate mirror for a bit longer each day, eventually, you would start to feel more comfortable. You would start to recognize certain parts of the image being reflected. You would even notice that when you return to the fun house mirror, you no longer feel comfortable. You may start to question it. When people compliment parts of you that you can now see in the image reflected by the accurate mirror, you may start to accept and believe these compliments. This is how it works when using your corrected belief.

Chapter 25

Learn to Accept Other People's Good Opinion of You

Courtney was referred to me by her long-term individual therapist. She felt stuck helping Courtney disengage from her deeply entrenched anxiety rooted in the distorted belief that she is broken and incapable. Courtney's distorted belief impacted many aspects of her life.

At the end of one of my early sessions with Courtney, she said to me, "I'm worried that I am not broken enough for you to be seeing me. Your time is valuable, and I don't know if you should be using it on me."

In the moment, I responded, "Your time is as valuable as mine. And I can hear how much you're affected by anxiety in your day-to-day life. I'm glad you're here to work on it."

At our next session, feeling that I might have missed an opportunity to respond adequately to that statement, I brought it up again.

"I want to check in with you to see how you felt after you shared with me your worry that your problems aren't serious enough to take my time."

Looking slightly uncomfortable, Courtney smiled and said, "I beat myself up about that for days. I worried you thought it was a stupid thing for me to say."

I used this moment to observe Courtney's distorted belief in action, recognizing her question as a reflection of her fear that she wasn't good enough to deserve my time and attention. I saw her reaction to my affirming response—beating herself up for saying something 'stupid'—as an attempt to maintain her negative self-image despite my positive response

At one point in our conversation, Courtney said to me, "If you thought it was stupid, it's not like you would tell me so."

I smiled, "You're right, I wouldn't. But if there was something about what you said that I thought we should look at, I would find a way to do that. And it's also true that I'm never going to say something I don't mean. Can I share with you what I thought when you said that to me in our last session?"

Courtney looked nervous but agreed.

"I thought it was incredibly helpful that you shared that worry with me. I was so impressed with you that you could say out loud what you were thinking and feeling at that moment. That is doing therapy at a master level. It gave us both an opportunity to see your anxiety in action, in real time".

Courtney was silent. She looked uncomfortable. After a couple of moments, she said, "You just completely took away any way for me to discount what you said. I don't know what to do. I want to accept your feedback but I'm also intensely uncomfortable."

Courtney perfectly articulated the experience of trying to allow for a new and corrected reality or belief. Even if the new belief is a positive one – I would say especially when the new belief is a positive one – its unfamiliarity will feel intensely uncomfortable. The intensity of the discomfort will be proportionate to your attachment to the false belief.

I said, "See if you can sit in this moment of having nowhere to hide, and if you can make even a little bit of space for my experience of you."

I suggested that Courtney try on the thought, "It is okay for me to feel uncomfortable while I consider this new possibility." For a few minutes in our session, Courtney was able to do just that, and she could allow herself to feel the sincerity of my words and consider a new self-image. This alone did not change her overall belief. But along with many other similarly small victories, it became a building block to a new way of seeing herself.

This exchange in my session with Courtney exemplifies another essential ingredient in the process of correcting a distorted belief – the ability to accept another's positive experience of you when it differs from your own self-perception.

Changing a long-held belief about yourself is hard work. I have already described the ways you likely cling to false beliefs about yourself by rejecting and deflecting the world's positive view of you. This positive view is mirrored back to you through compliments and feedback, highlighting your strengths and the qualities others value and appreciate.

How do you typically respond when you receive a compliment? Do you feel a warm sense of recognition and appreciation that someone has noticed a quality or ability you recognize in yourself? Do you experience a feeling of pride or maybe gratitude? Or do you feel uncomfortable and find a way to distance yourself from the compliment or reject it altogether?

My wish is for you to know the feeling of warmth, appreciation, pride and gratitude when receiving compliments or praise. I also wish for you to see it as a reflection of something you know to be true and appreciate others noticing, not in an arrogant way, but in a humble way. Those with anxiety from distorted beliefs often worry that if they think well of themselves or accept compliments, they will become arrogant and self-centered. I can honestly say I have never seen someone go from being overly self-deprecating and self-loathing to arrogant. Doing so would require a personality overhaul.

When you receive a compliment, see if you can pause to reflect on the compliment, accept it, and internalize it. Internalizing it is bringing the compliment from the outside to within, where you hold it as an affirmation of a truth. Can you stop and consider that whatever admiration is being conveyed to you reflects something true? Can you receive and accept the compliment without minimizing or deflecting it? If doing any of this sounds hard, can you at least accept that the compliment being given is true to the person giving it, even if you do not recognize it yourself? You might say to yourself, "I accept that this is how X sees me and feels about me." This is what Courtney was tasked with doing when receiving my feedback about her use of therapy.

David Burns, a renowned Cognitive Behavioral Therapist and author of the book, *Feeling Good, The New Mood Therapy* has been known to direct his clients who struggle to accept compliments to say in response to receiving one, "I'm sorry, but I just can't let you think that about me." His purpose in doing so is to say out loud what one is silently enacting by rejecting or deflecting a compliment. To say this out loud is an absurd response to a compliment, and it is designed to make you aware of the absurdity of the automatic defense against other people's positive experiences of you.

Chapter 26

How Changing Your Behaviors Can Change Your Beliefs

Julia was a kind, highly likable, smart, capable young woman. She came to therapy to address pervasive anxiety and depression rooted in the false and distorted belief that she was inadequate/not good enough. Her anxiety manifested in numerous ways, including avoiding situations where attention would be focused on her, feeling awkward in social situations, and feeling the need to rehearse how she would interact with others because she feared she wouldn't know how to seem "normal." She rarely voiced preferences for what she wanted to do or where she wanted to go – including with her loving, supportive partner. For instance, she never suggested a restaurant she wanted to go to without first looking up the menu and making sure there were items she anticipated he would want to order. If asked by him where she wanted to go for dinner, she routinely chose places she thought he would pick rather than where she wanted to go. She instinctively always placed other's needs in front of her own, a behavior she had long ago adopted to compensate for her perceived inadequacy.

Julia had many talents, including baking and cooking. When she baked items and brought them to work, they would be devoured in minutes with effusive compliments from her coworkers. A friend asked her to bake her wedding cake. While Julia could recognize the response to her cooking and baking, she simultaneously deflected it. She would respond to compliments with disclaimers as to why the food had not turned out as well as it could have or why it may not be very good. I observed this pattern and identified it as a way to keep the compliments at a distance.

Having named this behavior, we worked on changing it. During one of our sessions, Julia shared that she had friends coming over for dinner that night. This provided an opportunity for her to practice new behavior. I tasked Julia with serving the food without any disclaimers or explaining why it might not be very good. If she received any compliments on the food, I encouraged her to simply say, "Thank you. I'm glad you like it." This felt foreign and uncomfortable to Julia, so much so that we role-played and rehearsed this scenario in our session.

The following week, Julia returned to therapy and shared that she had successfully completed her homework assignment, doing exactly as we had rehearsed. While she admitted feeling uncomfortable and awkward at first, she also noted that it helped her be more open to her friends' positive reactions to the meal she had prepared.

A few months later, Julia shared the following story with me. "I was having some friends over, and I baked a cake. When I removed the cake layers from the cake pans, one of them got stuck, and the cake broke apart. I took the one layer that came out whole and frosted and decorated it. My friends were sitting in the living room, and when I brought the cake out to them from the kitchen, I said, 'Look how cute this little cake is!'"

I stopped Julia. "Wait, can we pause here for a moment? Do you realize what just happened?"

"No, what happened?"

"If that had happened 6 months or a year ago, what would you have done?"

Julia stopped to reflect for a moment and then said with surprise, "Oh! I would have started over and baked a whole new cake!"

"I know! You never would have served a cake that was not "perfect." Not only did you not start over when the cake stuck to the pan, but as you were carrying this half cake out to your friends, you said, 'Look how cute this little cake is!' That is amazing!"

Julia had not consciously done this. Her telling of this story had little to do with what she wanted to talk about in therapy. There had been no forethought or effort put into her decision to go ahead and serve the "imperfect" cake or in her proclaiming, as she carried it out to her friends, "Look how cute this little cake is!"

This is the nature of change when you consciously shift behavior that is attached to distorted beliefs. When you start, it will feel uncomfortable and unfamiliar. It may feel so difficult that it seems impossible. You may need support, encouragement, and practice before you feel able to do it. It likely will not change the way you feel in the moment. But over time, when repeated, it can take hold in ways that will start to feel natural and effortless. Sometimes, you won't even notice it as it becomes internalized!

Return to the list you created of the behaviors you engage in because of your distorted belief. As you develop awareness of more behaviors, add them to the list. For each behavior you list, I want you to consider how that behavior would change or look different if you believed your corrected belief. For example, I have challenged myself to go to numerous events by myself that I may have otherwise avoided by focusing on the thought, "I can handle going alone and talking with people I don't know," rather than focusing on the fear that I might feel awkward. How would you act differently if you knew your corrected belief was true? Write these new behaviors or actions down.

Each behavior you identify is an opportunity to practice acting in alignment with your corrected belief rather than your default distorted belief. Each time you engage in a new behavior, be sure to pay close attention to what happens. What is the outcome? How does it feel?

Like all other forms of anxiety discussed in this book, the work of changing your distorted beliefs requires both intention and repetition. You must actively and consciously work on catching yourself in your distorted belief, correcting it, and purposefully practicing new behavior. It requires patience and persistence. Patience – because change happens slowly and incrementally. You have likely lived with your distorted beliefs for most of your life. They have had years if not decades to become deeply rooted and entrenched. Persistence – because you may feel defeated when you do not make progress as quickly as you would like or when you experience the inevitable setbacks that we all do. Change never happens linearly. In reality, it looks much messier. Your job is only to trust the process, even when it is messy.

Noelle McWard Aquino

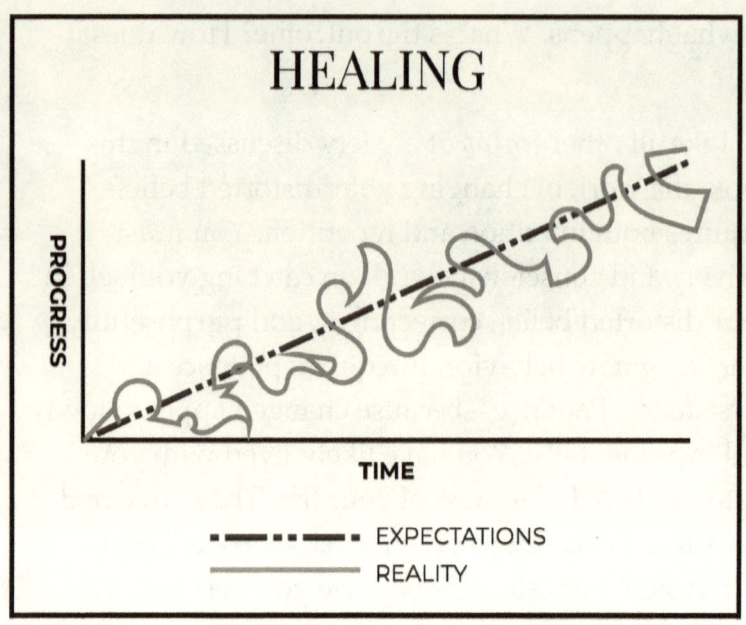

Chapter 27

Developing
Self-Compassion

M any who suffer from anxiety caused by distorted beliefs are intensely self-critical. In gaining mastery over your anxiety, it is essential to shift from self-hatred to self-compassion. Self-compassion is the practice of treating yourself with kindness, care, and empathy, particularly in times of struggle and difficulty. It includes being self-forgiving when you make a mistake and accepting your flaws by recognizing that everyone has them. Being imperfect is part of the human condition, and everyone has some aspects of themselves that at times make them feel inadequate or shameful.

Self-compassion involves extending the same compassion, empathy, and support to you that you would offer to a dear friend or loved one. A common characteristic of the objection used by distorted belief is to have one set of criteria for judging and criticizing yourself that does not apply to anyone else in your life.

Everyone else is worthy of kindness and compassion, while you and you alone are not. Self-compassion seeks to make you equal to others – not better, not worse, but one with.

Kristin Neff, a psychologist and the author of *Self-Compassion: The Proven Power of Being Kind to Yourself* identifies three components to self-compassion.

1. **Mindfulness:** Being aware and present with your thoughts, feelings, and sensations without judgment or avoidance. Mindfulness can help you acknowledge and accept your emotions without being overwhelmed by them.
2. **Common Humanity:** Recognizing that experiencing pain, failure, or challenges is a normal and universal part of the human experience. Understanding that you are not alone in your struggles can foster a sense of connection and empathy towards yourself and others.
3. **Self-Kindness:** Being warm, understanding, and gentle towards yourself, especially in moments of pain or difficulty. It means responding to your own suffering with kindness and nurturing rather than harsh self-criticism or judgment.

To practice self-compassion, first consider a situation that is causing you stress or to feel badly about yourself. Notice what feelings arise or what sensations you have in your body. Allow yourself to feel your feelings exactly as they are. This awareness of your emotions and physical discomfort is the mindfulness step of self-compassion. Write these feelings/sensations down. For example, you may notice feeling:

- Embarrassment
- Shame
- Anxiety
- Sadness

Next, acknowledge that suffering, mistakes or disappointment are a part of life. This is the human experience. It is what Kristin Neff refers to as common humanity. Write down what you are feeling upset or disappointed by and then add a statement such as:

- Other people feel this way too.
- We all struggle in our lives.
- I am not alone in my feelings or experience.
- Making mistakes is human.

Lastly, what do you need to hear to be kind to yourself? Consider a statement that invites you to be gentle, compassionate, and supportive towards yourself. You might consider:

- May I grow to accept myself as I am.
- I forgive myself.
- I am doing the best I can.
- It is okay to feel as I do – there is nothing wrong with me or what I am feeling.

- I do not need to be perfect to have value and goodness.
- Mistakes are an opportunity to grow and learn.

Another practice around self-compassion can be to write yourself a letter or a dialogue between yourself and a wise, loving other. Write to yourself as the voice of a friend who loves you dearly. What would they say to you about the stressful situation? Alternatively, you can write to yourself as if you were writing to a friend who you love and respect, imagining that they are the ones who have the problem or worry. What would you say to them? After writing this letter or dialogue, read it whenever you are feeling anxious or critical.

A final practice for cultivating self-compassion is to reflect on the first time you remember being critical or judgmental toward yourself. How old were you? What were you thinking and feeling about yourself in that moment? Try to visualize yourself at that age — or better yet, find a picture of yourself from that time. Then, imagine speaking directly to that younger version of you. What do you most want them to know? What words would they most need to hear? Make this a regular habit: connecting with and comforting the younger you who first experienced the seeds of the feelings you carry today.

Sally was a competent, likable, funny woman with a strong work ethic who was extremely self-critical. When she perceived that she had made a mistake, she amplified the impact of it and viewed any mistake (often inconsequential) as proof that she was a failure. Any error resulted in rumination on the mistake and harsh self- criticism and anxiety over a feared impact of the mistake that rarely, if ever, materialized. She often berated herself with recriminations of being "an idiot". If others suggested that she'd made an error, she would become highly reactive and defensive, often experiencing the feedback in magnified negative ways.

The mistakes that were often most impactful were those made at work. Constructive feedback or differences in the approach to doing the job between Sally and her coworkers often became the focus of rumination and emotional distress. She would either become highly reactive to coworkers or supervisors if she perceived them as being critical of her, which was a defensive stance against her sensitivity to making a mistake. Or she would beat herself up and over-generalize or exaggerate the impact of an error.

With either reaction, our work in therapy focused on normalizing making mistakes, putting them into perspective, and practicing self-compassion around being an imperfect human being, as we all are.

Over time, Sally began to experience greater emotional stability and resilience. Whereas early in therapy, when her mood often shifted from one session to the next between anxiety and depression, she gradually began to report and demonstrate a more steadily consistent and positive mood. When the typical frustrations arose at work, she became less reactive to them. She became more accepting of her own imperfections by recognizing and holding her strengths while acknowledging her mistakes and normalizing them. She also became more tolerant of others by not overly personalizing feedback or other's personality traits and idiosyncrasies.

During a lengthy period of noticeably improved emotional stability and mood, Sally shared two stories in the same session, which beautifully demonstrated her ability to successfully implement self-compassion. In one, she admitted to letting down a friend who was counting on her for help she had agreed to provide. On the day of the promised assistance, she realized that she would no longer be available.

She shared with me, "I immediately apologized, recognizing that I had let her down. I made no excuses for it and didn't try to manage her feelings about it. I just acknowledged that she had been counting on me, that I let her down, and I was sorry." Sally went on to say, "I was unsure how much time I should give her before checking in on her again. A friend encouraged me to do so sooner rather than later, so I did that night, and she responded right away. She accepted my apology, and we are okay."

Sally was calm throughout the story. Absent were the tears, self-recrimination, and self-loathing that would have been present earlier in therapy. In its place was the ability to acknowledge and own her mistake, to feel appropriately (not disproportionately) regretful and apologetic and to communicate this to her friend in a way that was sincere. She was able to see the situation for what it was; a mistake that negatively impacted her friend and which she regretted, not an indictment on herself as a person.

The second story Sally shared involved a mistake she made at work over which her supervisor expressed frustration. When describing the situation, Sally said, "I did mess that up. And I forgive myself. My boss was irritated, and I know he is worried that I will make a mistake again on this important report coming up. I want to tell him I know what I got wrong, and that he doesn't have to worry; I won't make that mistake again. I understand the importance of the report and my assignment."

I had become so accustomed to Sally berating herself for any mistake she made that to hear her say, "I forgive myself" was monumental. It was moving to witness the calm and steadiness with which she could own the mistake, accept her supervisor's reaction to it, and her confidence in reassuring him that she could still be trusted and relied on.

Chapter 28

**Risking Vulnerability
As a Path to Knowing
Your True Self**

Self-compassion can be further developed by sharing
your vulnerable feelings and perceived challenges
or shortcomings (often based in your distorted beliefs)
with others. Brene Brown promotes self-compassion
when she speaks about embracing vulnerability and
imperfection as a path to courageous and wholehearted
living. She champions welcoming and accepting
imperfections as strengths which make you more
authentically human and allows for deeper connection
with others and personal growth.

When you pause to reflect on the moments in your
life when you felt truly seen, understood, and
meaningfully connected to others, you'll likely find they
were the times when you allowed yourself to be
vulnerable.

For instance, many of my clients express feelings of
embarrassment or shame about being in therapy, often
keeping it a secret from those around them. However,
when they gather the courage to reveal this to others,

they are met with support and empathy. Surprisingly, those they confide in often open up about their own experiences with therapy, revealing a shared connection that was previously unknown. In every case, my clients experienced a deeper sense of connection with those they confided in. They also felt more seen, accepted, and a sense of kinship with others.

I recall an impactful conversation I had with a colleague. He shared with me that years before, his wife had died while they were in the process of divorcing. He attended a grief support group, where for many months he shared his experiences of grief. One day, he took a risk and shared with the group feelings of relief related to her passing; describing the pain he felt in their unhealthy dynamics. In response to his sharing, many of the other group members opened up about their own conflicted feelings because of challenges they experienced in their relationships with the person they were grieving. Until he was brave enough to give voice to these feelings that might be considered taboo, or for which he feared he would be judged, everyone else remained silent about their own suffering. Once he shared these vulnerable feelings, he was met with a sense of shared humanity, support and connection, which gave everyone in the room permission to be more authentic.

It is common for those who struggle with negatively distorted beliefs to hide their stressors and challenges from others. I commonly hear people express not wanting to be a burden as the reason for internalizing rather than sharing. They are quick to point out that their friends and family have their own challenges to deal with and do not need to be further encumbered with their problems. This is often a coping mechanism to their perceived inadequacy that serves to perpetuate it.

If your distorted belief is one of perceived inadequacy or unworthiness, you may seek to build relationships by focusing on the other person's needs while never sharing your own. When this is your coping strategy, at best, it keeps you at a distance from your friends and family. At worst, it breeds resentment, largely because you participate in relationships in a one-sided way, keeping your needs and wants unexpressed. Taking risks to express your needs, wants, or to say no to requests that do not work for you can be a form of being more vulnerable.

Margaret was a mother to three school-aged children who was actively involved as a volunteer at her children's school. She also supported her husband's business by handling his bookkeeping and other administrative tasks. Her life centered on taking care of and supporting others. The only thing she did exclusively for herself was attend therapy for one hour a week. She often referred to it as a sacred time she looked forward to.

One week, an hour before her session, Margaret called to cancel her appointment. She told me that something had come up and she was unable to make it, adding that she understood I would need to charge her because of the short notice.

When Margaret came in the next week, she explained that a friend had called her that morning to ask a favor. Her friend's babysitter was sick and unable to come to work. Margaret's friend had an appointment to attend and asked Margaret to watch her children for her. Margaret said yes.

A theme of Margaret's therapy was anxiety and depression that stemmed from an underdeveloped sense of self. Margaret was the youngest of 8 children and was significantly younger than her siblings. She described her parents as loving but "tired", and she often felt overlooked. She lacked a sense of her own qualities, skills, and personality, and she struggled to know her uniqueness and where she fit in. Her way of getting attention and feeling like she was a part of things was to be a people pleaser, accommodating the needs of others. She saw herself only in relationship to others and attending to their needs.

When Margaret shared with me the reason for her cancellation the week before, I asked her, "Margaret, when your friend called to ask you to watch her children, did any part of you consider telling her that as much as you would like to help, you would not be able to because you had an appointment scheduled for yourself that morning?"

"No, I never thought to say that" was her reply.

"In saying yes, not only did you sacrifice something that is important to you, but you also assumed the burden of having to pay for the appointment."

"I know. I realized that, but only later, after I had said yes."

"If the roles were reversed, and you had called this friend and she had told you no because she had an appointment scheduled that day, how would you have reacted?"

"I would have completely understood! I wouldn't have been upset at all."

"How would you have felt if she had said yes, and you later found out that in doing so, she had canceled and paid for an appointment that she had scheduled for herself that day?"

Margaret paused for a moment and her face registered a pained recognition. "I would feel terrible. I would never want anyone to do that."

"No, you wouldn't. And I can only assume that she would not have wanted you to either. You matter. Your needs matter. And I want to support you in your discovery of this truth by taking risks to say no when you need to, and to experience others understanding and supporting you in doing so."

This session was a turning point for Margaret. She began to take risks to say no to some requests and to be more authentic in her relationships with others. She was met with genuine support and care each time she did, which reinforced her ability to keep doing so. This led her to take more risks by expressing her wants, needs and preferences. This helped her to begin to form a new self-image that saw herself as worthy and deserving of friendship and love.

When your family and friends share their struggles, insecurities, and fears with you, you likely feel closer to them. You no doubt feel honored or special that they trust you enough to confide in you. When you withhold your feelings of vulnerability or your need for support and help from others, you rob them of the opportunity to feel special and important in your life. And you block both you and them from feeling closer.

If you shy away from being vulnerable with others, this is an area of practice for you. Taking risks by sharing vulnerability will help you to learn new things about yourself by observing and receiving the way you are responded to by others. It will also help you connect with others in deeper and more meaningful ways, which can also be transformative in how you see yourself. To help you with this practice, consider the following steps.

1. **Choose a family member or friend** who is safe emotionally and with whom you feel comfortable. Trust is crucial when it comes to vulnerability because you want to feel confident that the person you open up to will respond with empathy and support. Do not choose someone

240

who has historically been unreliable in their ability to provide it.

2. **Reflect on a challenge you are facing** or a need or wish you want to express. Identify the feelings attached to this challenge, need or want. This self-awareness of your emotions will help you to more effectively communicate.

3. **Start small by sharing something that feels manageable** and not overwhelmingly personal or vulnerable. This will help you to practice and gain confidence before moving to more personal or deeper aspects of yourself.

4. **Share your emotions.** When opening up to someone, be sure to communicate not just the details of an event that happened, but also how you feel about what happened. Telling a story is not showing vulnerability. Sharing how you felt within the story is. If you are making a request or asking for help, share your emotions surrounding this request.

5. **Be open to receiving.** Pay attention to how your friend or family member responds to you. If you are shown kindness, care or empathy, seek to notice and feel this. If a request is granted, receive the care for you this demonstrates. Watch out for feelings of guilt, or anything else that might block your full acceptance of the care, empathy or kindness extended to you.

6. **Accept the outcome.** If you feel disappointed in how you are responded to, understand that not

everyone will respond to your vulnerability in the way you hope. People have their own limitations. The goal of sharing your vulnerability is to foster deeper and more authentic connections with others, and to come to know yourself in a new way through these connections.

Revealing your vulnerability is a powerful way to discern individuals who are genuinely supportive and trustworthy in your life, as opposed to those who may not be. Practicing sharing vulnerability incrementally can help you to focus on the healthiest and most reciprocal relationships in your life.

Whenever reflecting on the topic of vulnerability, I think about one of the most beautiful moments of my life that coincided with one of the most painful and vulnerable.

Before sharing this story, it might be helpful to know more about my relationship with vulnerability. Feedback I have received from close friends over the years is that I always appear to be strong and that I "have it all together." Some of this perception is due to my historical avoidance of showing vulnerability. This traces back to the themes of feeling shy and not wanting to be seen as "needy" that have woven throughout my life. In the past, I had friends articulate that at times, this lack of showing vulnerability felt like a barrier to greater closeness. They voiced that my being more vulnerable also made me more human and relatable.

One of the most painful and vulnerable experiences of my life was going through a divorce. In the earliest stages of the process, I instinctively reached out to others for support. The first people I sought out were friends who had been through this painful experience.

One of the first people I reached out to was Sarah, someone I had known for years but with whom at the time I did not have a close, personal relationship. In fact, my only contact information for Sarah was through Facebook. To reach out to her was an act of vulnerability to begin with. I sent her a private message which she responded to immediately. Within a day or two, we were meeting for breakfast. This became a regular event, meeting for breakfast every few weeks, often at her initiation. Sarah checked in on me frequently and offered tremendous support and advice.

One of the single most painful moments of the process was telling our children that their father and I were getting a divorce. He and I planned when and how we would tell them. I shared with Sarah at one of our breakfasts how filled with anxiety and dread I was about having this conversation. I was vulnerable with her. Sarah later texted me and said, "I want to ask you to do something. Right before you tell the kids, would you text me the word 'now' so that I will know it is happening, and I can stop whatever I am doing to send you love and positive energy? In fact, I have a vision of you having an army of people praying for you and holding you in love and support at that moment, all getting the text that says 'now.'"

This remains one of the most touching and meaningful offers of support I have received in my life.

I took Sarah's invitation and suggestion and asked my closest friends to receive this text. At the designated time, I sent a text to a group of friends that simply said, "Now." Though I did not see their responses until after the conversation, I knew and could feel that I had this "army" of support with me, holding my children and me in love. I will forever be grateful to Sarah for this simple but profound gesture. And I am aware that I would never have been gifted with such meaningful support had I not been willing or able to expose my vulnerability.

Chapter 29

Draw Attention to What Makes You Anxious

A final strategy for attending to anxiety stemming from distorted beliefs is to call attention to the thing that you perceive as your shortcoming. As discussed in Chapter 2, the most common human response to anxiety is avoidance. If your anxiety is based on a negatively distorted belief, you will likely seek to hide from others certain aspects of yourself - or even avoid being visible - due to these false perceptions. If, instead, you bring attention to what makes you feel uncomfortable or self-conscious, you may find that, paradoxically, your anxiety often lessens or even disappears.

Allison, a young woman with severe social anxiety, shared with me her experience attending a bridal shower for one of her close friends. Allison felt intense anxiety leading up to the shower. Even though the bride-to-be was one of her best friends and she knew many of the other guests invited, she still anticipated feeling awkward, uncomfortable and unsure of herself interacting with the other guests. While at the shower, she met a woman who appeared to be completely at ease and who was engaging and interactive with many of the guests. When the time came for everyone to be seated at tables for a meal, this guest said to Allison and others around her, "Now comes the part where I awkwardly pick a table and hope that other people will come and sit with me." This was exactly how Allison felt too. To hear this guest, who Allison experienced as dynamic and socially comfortable, say out loud what she herself was thinking and feeling, immediately put her at ease. In fact, all the women who heard the comment shared feeling similarly awkward about choosing a table and seat. When Allison shared this story with me, I noted that not only was she put at ease by the guest saying this, but undoubtedly the guest was as well. She named her anxiety out loud and in doing so, likely greatly relieved or eliminated it for herself.

Naming and declaring your fear out loud disempowers your anxiety and will often engender support from and connection with others. I attended a concert at the end of the lockdown phase of the pandemic. The opening act announced from the stage, "This is my first time performing in two years and I am nervous tonight." The audience responded by applauding and cheering him on.

Ruth, a young woman who suffered from severe social anxiety despite her excellent social skills and likeability, often displayed physical signs of her anxiety by getting red, flushed, and sweaty in social situations.

246

This heightened her anxiety about socializing except with her closest friends, causing her to avoid most social situations.

Part of Ruth's work on her social anxiety was to engage, rather than avoid, and to draw attention to these physical signs of her anxiety when they arose. If, in a social situation, she became red and flushed, Ruth practiced saying, "I get red very easily, which is kind of embarrassing for me, but don't worry, I'm fine and it will pass." Or, "Am I red right now? I flush so easily!"

This understandably felt uncomfortable at first, as it required drawing attention to the thing that was most embarrassing for her and which she most wanted to avoid. Yet she did her homework and was amazed by how quickly the anxiety attached to her blushing dissipated by simply drawing attention to it. Each time she did, people responded to her with kindness or shared discomfort which made her feel accepted; red face and all. In fact, drawing attention to this source of embarrassment was so effective that after doing so two or three times, it ceased to be an issue of concern for her. She continued to flush at times, but she stopped feeling self- conscious about it.

Recalling the story of my inability to speak while guest lecturing in the law school class, what stopped my anxiety and enabled me to continue speaking was naming out loud to the class what was happening to me - I was experiencing the very same symptoms of anxiety I was describing to them. As soon as I drew attention to what was obviously happening, the anxiety dissipated, and I was able to continue speaking normally.

The next time you are feeling anxious, try naming it out loud and see what happens. You might be surprised by how it transforms your anxiety.

Chapter 30

Case Study: Monica

Monica came to therapy as a recently divorced mother of three children. She was at peace with her divorce but wanted to better understand her role in the marriage and its ultimate ending, in part to avoid repeating unhealthy patterns in future relationships. She was successful in her career, had a strong support network of friends, and was actively involved in volunteering. Despite her outwardly successful life, Monica often felt sad and struggled to fully enjoy her life. Though she loved her children deeply, she often felt stressed as a parent, particularly in parenting her middle child, who was on the autism spectrum.

Underlying Monica's presenting issues were anxiety and mild depression stemming from distorted beliefs. Monica saw herself as fundamentally flawed - believing herself to be so deeply inadequate that she felt compelled to take up as little space as possible. This self-concept was so deeply internalized that Monica did not question its accuracy or validity. To her, it was simply an accepted fact. She was convinced that if she was seen by others in any significant way, they too would discover how flawed she is and would reject her.

Monica was the younger of two children. Her father was the oldest of seven and according to Monica, his was a childhood filled with abuse. His father was a severe alcoholic who was physically abusive. Being the oldest, her father would try to protect his younger siblings by seeking to redirect his father's anger away from them and towards himself, thereby bearing the brunt of his father's abuse. As a parent, Monica's father was highly critical of her and her brother and controlling in his expectations and demands of them. Monica believed she was a constant disappointment to her father. She was not athletic, something he valued and forced on her and her brother, nor a natural student in school. While Monica could identify her father's behavior as sometimes harsh and critical, she downplayed its impact on her since it did not look like the abuse he had suffered at the hands of his father.

Having internalized the belief that she was deeply flawed, Monica developed many behaviors to compensate for this belief. She was passive in relationships and reluctant to identify needs or wants while being very accommodating of others. Her dating history was filled with relationships with unavailable men, in large part due to her distorted belief that given her own inadequacy, she should not expect much from them.

Though she was successful and well regarded at work, she saw herself through the lens of the things she was challenged by in her job rather than being able to own and internalize her competencies and skills. She downplayed her competencies or credited others for her successes.

A first step in therapy was helping Monica to name her internalized self-belief, and to frame it as false and distorted. This was ongoing work as the belief in her fundamental inadequacy impacted all aspects of her life. Early on, Monica struggled to accept that her self-perception was faulty.

"I know you keep saying that I am not seeing myself accurately, but it feels true to me."

"I know it feels true. But just because you feel it is true, doesn't mean that it is. If your daughter came to you and said that she feels stupid and incapable when something in school doesn't make sense to her right away, would you agree with her that she is?"

"No, of course not! But that's different. She's a child. She's still learning."

"Can you remember yourself as a child, maybe at the same age that your daughter is now?"

"Yes."

"When your father was critical of you back then, what did that look like? What would he say and do?"

Monica was very still, thinking, and then quietly said, "He would get angry and yell. He would tell me what I had done wrong or needed to do better. If it was about sports, he would make me practice over and over again until I got it right - though I wasn't always able to do what he wanted me to do. He would get very frustrated when it was about school, like he couldn't understand why I didn't get something."

"How do you remember feeling in those moments?"

"Scared. Stupid. Like a failure."

"And what did you do in those moments when you felt scared and like a failure?"

"I tried to make him happy. I tried to do and be what he wanted. I got quiet. My brother would fight back, but I just got quiet."

"Yes, like maybe if you just got it right and were quiet enough, he would stop yelling at you. He would stop focusing on you and what was wrong with you."

Monica nodded quietly, "Yes".

"Much like you do now."

Monica was quiet for a long moment, tears silently falling down her cheeks, and then nodded, "Yes. I see that."

Monica focused on identifying her distorted beliefs and the behaviors they triggered as they unfolded in real time. While building her capacity to recognize these patterns, we also worked on internalizing what was in fact true about her. Monica was highly likable, smart, thoughtful, kind, creative, and charismatic. People were drawn to her and liked her. She had many friends and was clearly valued and well regarded at work. One of the goals of therapy was to help Monica recognize her many talents, qualities and skills while holding them alongside her imperfections. Having weaknesses did not cancel out her strengths.

Another focus in therapy was her dating relationships. Monica was active in dating post-divorce, and this provided an opportunity to observe the familiar dynamics of expecting little from those she dated and having few needs within her relationships. As Monica went on dates, she learned to be more attuned to her feelings. Her old pattern was to dismiss and rationalize away things that did not feel good. In therapy, with a more attuned connection to her genuine feelings, she worked to align her behavior with these feelings. When encountering unreliable or unavailable men, she more quickly ended those relationships. The act of ending a relationship itself was new behavior. She took risks asking for what she wanted and to be open to receiving from others without feeling guilty. This work led her to a fulfilling and healthy relationship with a man to whom she is now engaged.

Monica's negatively distorted self-view also extended to how she perceived herself as a parent. She struggled with one of her children's frequently challenging behaviors. Monica would receive phone calls from her daughter's school that her daughter was speaking out impulsively, talking back to teachers, or being disruptive to fellow students. At home, she would challenge Monica's authority. As a parent, Monica felt like a failure. She worried if her children, her daughter in particular, would become good citizens as adults. She assumed that teachers and fellow parents were judging her based on the behavior of her children.

While normalizing and validating the parenting challenges that accompanied her daughter's behavior, the work of therapy focused on Monica's negative self-view as a parent. I routinely reflected to Monica all the ways she responded to her daughter's behavior with patience, thoughtful discussion, empathy, and a sense of accountability. When contacted by her daughter's school, she responded by taking the complaints seriously, not making excuses for them, and partnering with the school to address the issues. Monica sought resources and support for her daughter through therapy and testing to understand the root of the problematic behavior. When she was diagnosed with ADHD and high-functioning autism, Monica put in place additional resources to help support her and manage her symptoms. All of this was reflected back to challenge Monica's internal belief that she had failed as a parent. I often reminded Monica that when it comes to parenting, no approach that works some of the time works all the time. And we often don't see the immediate results of the work we put in now; rather, the true impact of that work becomes visible only further down the road. We worked on helping Monica to see herself as a parent in more accurate and self-compassionate ways, while simultaneously building her capacity to trust that the impact of all she attempted to do now could be realized in the future.

Therapy also focused on how Monica struggled to relate to her daughter because her behaviors were different from Monica's childhood behaviors. Monica came to understand that her high level of compliance and rule following was her way of managing her own anxiety as a child. This helped Monica to have more self-compassion and to understand why she felt so triggered and anxious when her daughter did not feel equally compelled to be compliant. Connecting her own compliance to her fear of her father allowed her to reframe her daughter's behavior through the lens of her own sense of safety with Monica.

As Monica became more accepting of herself, she also became more accepting of her daughter. Over time Monica reported feeling more relaxed, and as a result, sharing more time and experiences with her children that felt enjoyable and connected. Though she was always an attentive parent, she became able to genuinely have more fun with them. She found a new pleasure in family game nights and movie nights and felt more relaxed when her children bickered or were "loud," in contrast to her coping mechanism of being quiet in her quest to be invisible.

Monica's sense of self, and subsequently her quality of life and ability to enjoy it, blossomed in therapy. Her core distorted belief of being flawed and inadequate, and the default behavior of making herself as small and invisible as possible never fully left her. That's the nature of core beliefs - they remain a part of you. However, her ability to see herself more accurately and to trust this new image of herself took hold and shifted every aspect of her life in positive and inspiring ways.

Chapter 31

Review of Key Strategies for Distorted Beliefs

1. Accept and embrace what is true.

- Identify your core negative distorted belief.
- Identify behaviors you engage in because of this belief.
- Reflect on what past experiences informed your negatively distorted belief.
- Identify a replacement belief. This must be 100% believable and 100% true.

2. Accept other people's positive experience of you.

- Notice ways in which you deflect, reject or minimize compliments.
- Consciously work to accept that compliments reflect how you are seen/experienced by others.

3. Changing your behavior can change your beliefs.

- Each pattern of behavior you engage in because of your distorted belief is an opportunity to practice new behavior.

- Choose a behavior that lines up with your corrected belief and intentionally engage this new behavior.
- Pay attention to the outcome of practicing this new behavior.
- This requires patience, persistence and repetition.

4. Practice self-compassion

- Show yourself the same kindness, empathy and compassion you would extend to others.
- Practice the three components of self-compassion: mindfulness, common humanity, and self-kindness.
- Write a letter or a dialogue to yourself, speaking as you would someone you love.

5. Take risks and share your vulnerability with others

- Choose people in your life who are safe and likely to respond well to your vulnerability.
- Start small and build up to more personal/vulnerable sharing
- Share your feelings.
- Ask for help.
- Practice saying no.
- Be open to receiving from others.
- Accept the outcome.

6. Bring attention to what makes you anxious.

- Paradoxically, bringing attention to things that make you anxious can reduce or eliminate your anxiety.

260

Chapter 32

Conclusion

This book began with a story about my son. His story is ongoing. At the time of this writing, he still struggles with anxiety and obsessive-compulsive disorder. But it looks much different today than it did in the beginning. He understands the themes of his anxiety, the nature of the "lies" his brain habitually tells him, and he knows many things he can do for himself when he is feeling anxious. He is excellent at asking for help when he needs it, from a therapist, his family, his friends, or his college professors. He has identified many tools that help calm him when he is anxious. He knows his bad habits in response to anxiety, and though he does still fall into them at times, he works hard to break the habitual patterns that do not serve him. He is aided by medication, which is an essential tool in his toolkit. Over time, his episodes of intense anxiety have become fewer and far between, and when they emerge, last for a shorter time. Having anxiety and doing the work required to manage it has led him to be self-reflective and self-aware. Despite his anxiety, he takes risks (the good kind). He seeks to live a life with purpose. He is resilient.

There is a metaphor that comes from Acceptance and Commitment Therapy that beautifully captures a truth about anxiety. Emotions are like the waves in the ocean. Some waves are gentle, nothing more than a ripple. Others are choppy and turbulent. Some have the force and power of a tsunami, overwhelming everything in its path. Yet no matter how powerful and tempestuous the wave, it can never overpower the ocean itself. Eventually, all energy is reabsorbed back into the ocean, and the waves subside, returning to calm.

Anxiety is the wave. You are the ocean. Knowing how and why anxiety manifests for you personally, and using the tools described in this book that address the root of your anxiety will help you to navigate the intense waves of your anxiety and return to a state of calm and safety more easily.

I never promise complete freedom from anxiety. I do not believe this is a realistic or desired goal. Anxiety is a necessary emotion. At times, it is a wise one, alerting you to things that need your attention and care. Yet I do know that freedom from the weight and distress of your anxiety is achievable.

Understanding the root causes of your anxiety – whether it stems from catastrophizing, control, distorted belief, some combination of these, or all three

– is the first step in your journey from fear to freedom. Knowing the characteristics of your anxiety will give you powerful information to better understand how it operates in your system. Anticipating how the objections used by each root cause fights to preserve the anxiety will help you see through its convincing tactics and break free from its grip. Utilizing the tools and strategies outlined in this book that correspond with the root cause of your anxiety will aid you in creating more peace, calm, self-efficacy, and contentment.

Know that developing mastery over your anxiety is hard work. It requires patience, persistence and repetition. There is no such thing as curing your anxiety in simple, easy steps. I worry that if promises are made that the work is easy, it will lead to feeling discouraged or hopeless. Be kind to yourself. Look for small victories. Change happens one small moment at a time, moments that cumulatively create new ways of feeling and being.

There is a phrase coined by psychologist Donald Hebb which explains the concept of neuroplasticity. "Neurons that fire together wire together." It describes how neural pathways in the brain are formed and reinforced through repetition. Your anxiety patterns are the result of neurons that have fired together and wired together. The repetition of stimulus and response has created a super neural pathway, a superhighway if you will, in your brain – one that you enter automatically and travel with ease and rapid speed. Doing the work of transforming your anxiety is like building a brand-new road where none exists.

To build that road, you have to clear the land, dig the route, lay the gravel, pour the concrete and steamroll it into a smooth surface. All the while, the superhighway remains available for easy and speedy travel. While you are building the new road, it will always be easy to turn to the superhighway. Yet, each time you turn instead to the new road – the new response – neurons are firing together and wiring together. With enough repetition, they will grow in strength and the road you are building will take shape and become easy to travel. The more time you spend on the new road, the more it will become a well-worn path. And the more the old superhighway becomes less traveled, the more it will fall into disrepair.

It will develop potholes and cracks, and traveling on it will become less comfortable. Over time, as it falls into further neglect, weeds will appear and it will lose its appeal. The new road will take over as the superhighway. Both roads will always exist, and there will be times when, by habit, you will find yourself on the old road. When you do, you will discover it is no longer a comfortable road to travel, and you will seek to exit as quickly as possible.

While doing the work of transforming your anxiety, remember that you will still feel anxious and uncomfortable. You cannot wait until you don't feel anxious to start the work. Feelings are always the last thing to change. Remembering the universal truths of anxiety will help you to tolerate discomfort while you practice new ways of thinking and being. Breathing is essential. Your mind can focus on only one thought at a time, so focusing on a neutral or calming thought will aid you when stepping outside your comfort zone. Your impulse will be to avoid what makes you anxious. To truly free yourself from your anxiety, you must step into the anxiety rather than avoid it. When you are in an emotionally charged situation around things you do not know, your mind will fill in the blanks by making up a story – a story that represents your greatest fear and vulnerability. Your distress will likely stem more from the story than the facts. Remember: the story is almost never the truth of what is happening.

Seek support, whether that be from friends, family, or through therapy with a mental health professional. It can be hard to see habitual patterns or to know what other options exist and how to access them. One of the benefits of therapy is that it offers objective reflections of patterns in thoughts and behaviors that you may not be able to recognize yourself. Therapy provides support in understanding and healing the roots of those patterns, and guidance in adopting new ways of thinking and being in the world.

What I want most for you is to feel hope, knowing that it is possible to navigate the intricate paths of anxiety and to emerge on the other side stronger and more resilient. Every step taken, no matter how small, is a testament to your personal courage and capacity for growth. By embracing the journey, seeking support, cultivating new ways of thinking, experimenting with new ways of acting, and practicing patience and self-compassion, you will lay the path for transformation. By acknowledging the journey's difficulties while holding onto the belief that change is possible, you will transform the darkness of anxiety's shadows into the warmth and light of healing, contentment, peace and a deep appreciation for the strength that lies within.

In her poem, *I worried*, Mary Oliver wrote:

Finally, I saw that worrying came to nothing.

And gave it up. And took my old body

and went out into the morning,

and sang.

Let's go out and sing.

Afterword

An Interview With my Son
About Living and Making Peace With Anxiety

Me: How would you describe what it is like living with anxiety?

My Son: It affects pretty much every part of my life. It's like there is a radio in my head that gets tuned in to a bunch of different stations each day. Depending on what is happening externally, it will trigger different stations. Different things bring up different emotions. It's like having someone in the passenger seat at all times. You are never fully alone. There's always someone that is not necessarily controlling the reins but is whispering in your ear about what you should or shouldn't do. It's like having a devil and an angel on your shoulder.

Me: What would you say is the hardest thing about having anxiety?

My Son: Just the energy it takes. I have to do a lot of cognitive reframing to keep myself centered. I know logically what the truth is, but emotionally, internally, it's hard to tell sometimes. It's hard differentiating what's actually happening versus what my brain is making up and then having to do the work to center myself. It's like your brain is always going. You don't really have an off switch.

Me: Sometimes it's hard to tell the difference between what's true and what's not true?

My Son: Yeah.

Me: And sometimes you can know something is not true but still feel like it is?

My Son: Yes

Me: What is that like?

My Son: It's like you know you're doing something that you shouldn't be doing but you can't stop yourself. So, you watch yourself go down that path. It's somewhat out of body, like watching yourself from afar.

Me: What things have helped you the most with anxiety?

My Son: Therapy. Having friends who support me. Doing things that I enjoy or learning new skills - that helps my confidence. Putting myself in situations that are not very comfortable. There is a certain amount of rewiring you've got to do. Things that would have bothered me years ago no longer bother me [because I have pushed myself into doing things that are uncomfortable].

Me: Can you give me an example?

My Son: I used to be very rigid in my planning and time management. If things didn't happen exactly how I wanted or needed it to then I would spiral [into anxiety]. I felt like if I could not control that aspect then I would have no control at all. But now, I can let go of things much more easily, so I am not as locked in. Like at school or on projects I am working on, I am going to have to switch things around and sometimes I don't get to stuff and that's fine. I always get to the things I need to get to, but the order in which I do it doesn't matter as much anymore.

Me: How does it feel to have been able to change that?

My Son: It's good. It's helpful. Both my college experience, my career experience, everything I am trying to create for myself does not follow a linear path. Having an ability to adapt is really helpful. In any creative or business endeavor, things are not going to go as planned. Things will go wrong. Being able to switch gears has allowed me to keep going and to keep pursuing what I want.

Me: You said that therapy is one of the things that has helped you the most. What about therapy has been helpful to you?

My Son: It's a place to sort through the noise. There's a lot of noise, a lot of clutter. Having the space to pick it apart and learn coping skills has helped. It's a place to plan ahead for when things do happen, and you do get triggered. To identify what I can do to help myself in those situations.

Me: What coping skills have been most helpful for you?

My Son: Radical acceptance, cognitive reframing, distraction, movement. Honestly, the biggest thing is just letting it be. You can't change how you are feeling. I don't know if being okay with it is the right word, but to accept that that part of you [anxiety] is there. You may not be able to do anything about it right now, but anxiety doesn't have to drive the bus. It can sit in the back. You don't have to like it, but you don't have to try so hard to kick it out. Distraction has been a really big one too. It is what has helped me the most to not be controlled by my thoughts or feelings.

Me: In the book I talk about three types of anxiety that are rooted in different sources. They are catastrophizing, control and distorted beliefs. Where would you say your anxiety mostly comes from?

My Son: Control. I always try to control things externally. I've always been obsessed with controlling how the world unfolds before me. It then dips into catastrophizing and obsessing that bad things are going to happen [if things don't go the way I planned].

Me: Why do you think you do that [try to control things externally]?

My Son: It's a coping mechanism. During my formative years, I felt like I didn't have a lot of control at school, with friends. There was bullying at school, and then the divorce. Any control I can get now– it's like the kid in me trying to make up for that kid that didn't have control. Even though I have it now [control], I don't fully believe it. I'm always trying to make sure I retain it.

Me: Is there any way you have benefitted from or anything that you have gained because of anxiety?

My Son: I think I have had to fight a lot more than the average person. I've had to work through a lot of things, so it has given me a lot of resilience. There are some people who don't have it [anxiety] and the first time they get knocked down, it's hard for them to get back up. But I think I have been knocked down so many times, the only thing I know how to do is get back up. Also, I really care about everything I do. Everything I attempt and try to get better at, I usually do it with quite a bit of ferocity. I usually succeed in some form because I hold myself to such high standards. But that can also be a curse too. It's a blessing and a curse. It's my greatest strength and my biggest weakness at the same time. It's pushed me to work really hard. It's pushed me to be remarkable and to do really amazing things, mostly because I am scared of what would happen if I didn't. It's like a fire pushing me.

Me: What do you think would happen if you didn't push yourself so hard?

271

My Son: I think it would be a lot more sustainable. I've tried specifically to give myself a break and not let my goals get in the way of living. I made a promise that I would never let my goals supersede the things that matter. Like if I had to choose between doing something that made me happy or spending time with friends or indulging in things that fill my cup versus getting ahead in my aspirations or goals, I'd choose the first thing every time.

Me: Is there anything you want to say to people who are living with anxiety and maybe are just starting out on their journey?

My Son: It takes time. It doesn't happen overnight. I don't know if it ever ends fully, but it does get better. There's always something better ahead. It never stays the same unless you want it to stay the same. If you do the work, it will change. But you've got to be committed to doing the work. It sucks that you have to do the work, you shouldn't have to do the work, but that's the reality. It's either do the work or just stay where you are. Usually, it is more painful to stay where you are than to try to get better.

Acknowledgements

This book owes its existence to the unwavering support of numerous individuals, without whom, writing it would have been impossible. First and foremost is Ben, my biggest cheerleader and believer in the impact that this book can have on the lives of those living with anxiety. In my moments of questioning and doubt, he has been a source of unending support and patience. Writing this book took time and energy away from him, and my children – who have been nothing but supportive and encouraging. My son is the reason I care so deeply about trying to ease the suffering of those who live with anxiety. My daughter has been invaluable in helping to share my work through mediums I have little knowledge or practical skill with.

Marsha Craig has always held a bigger vision for what is possible through my work than any I have had for myself. And beyond her brilliance with all things marketing, she is the catalyst for my saying yes to writing a book.

Sara Connell, through her amazing generosity and incredible coaching program, Thought Leader

Academy, made every step of the writing and publishing process possible while also providing unending support and encouragement. And the many incredible women I met through this program who were, and are, a constant source of inspiration.

Special thanks to Mark Anthony Lord and Joan Coletto, who offered their homes for writing days and weekends. The dedicated time this carved out for writing, as well as the friendship, encouragement, and support contained within that space was a blessing I am deeply grateful for.

Hannah Rumsey, my editor, took my unpolished attempts at writing, and taught me to be more skillful as a writer and storyteller. I am amazed by the transformation of this book through her talents and guidance.

Tammy Letherer and Carol Dishell kindly agreed to be my beta readers. They were the first readers of the book in its completed form. To share something I had worked on for such a long time and could have kept trying to perfect indefinitely felt vulnerable. To share it with such safe and supportive friends who are each beautiful and accomplished writers was a gift. Their feedback, suggestions and support are appreciated immeasurably. Ann Sedgwick volunteered to read the book and support it (and me) through her amazing creative talents with branding and content promotion; and provided personal support and encouragement to me in moments of self-doubt.

And lastly, to my clients, whose stories I shared in the pages of this book. With the exception of those for whom I had no contact information, every client story has been shared with their permission. This is an act of generosity for which I am deeply grateful. What I know with certainty is that their stories will be not only relatable to the readers of this book but will serve to help others to take courageous steps in overcoming their anxiety. These clients and their stories are the heart and impact of this book.

Book Portal QR Code:

Access Bonus Content: Scan the QR code or visit the URL to access the book portal, where you'll find worksheets, exclusive videos, resources, and playlists to complement your experience with this book and further support your healing journey.

References

- Steimer, T. (2002). The biology of fear- and anxiety-related behaviors. *Dialogues in Clinical Neuroscience, 4*(3), 231–249. https://doi.org/10.31887/DCNS.2002.4.3/tsteimer

- No author. (2020, August 27). The biology of anxiety. *Psychology Today.* https://www.psychologytoday.com/us/basics/anxiety/the-biology- anxiety

- Curran, L. (2013). *Trauma competency: A clinician's guide.* PESI Publishing & Media.

- No author. (2020, July 6). Understanding the stress response. *Harvard Health Publishing.* https://www.health.harvard.edu/staying-healthy/understanding-the-stress-response

- Goleman, D. (2007). *Emotional intelligence* (10th ed.). Bantam Books.

- Sepalla, E. (2020, September 29). Research: Why deep breathing is so effective at reducing stress. *Harvard Business Review.*

https://hbr.org/2020/09/research-why-breathing-is-so-effective-at- reducing-stress

- Weil, A. (n.d.). Three breathing exercises and techniques. *Dr. Weil.* https://www.drweil.com/health-wellness/body-mind-spirit/stress-anxiety/breathing-three-exercises/

- Schwartz, J. M., & Bevette, B. (1996). *Brain lock: Free yourself from obsessive-compulsive behavior.* Harper Perennial.

- Burns, D. (1980). *Feeling good: The new mood therapy* (1st ed.). William Morrow and Company.

- Selva, J. (2017, January 31). Exploring the body-mind connection (Incl. 5 techniques). *Positive Psychology.* https://positivepsychology.com/body-mind-integration-attention-training/

- Crocket, R. (2024, March 4). How belly breathing benefits your body, mind. *Mayo Clinic Health System.* https://www.mayoclinichealthsystem.org/hometown-health/speaking-of- health/belly-breathing-benefits

- Agnihotri, A. (2024, July 13). 5 ways hugging supports your nervous system. *Hindustan Times.* https://www.hindustantimes.com/lifestyle/hea

lth/5-ways-hugging- supports-your-nervous-system-101663152229288.html

- van der Kolk, B. (2013, July 11). How trauma lodges in the body, revisited. *On Being with Krista Tippett.* https://onbeing.org/programs/bessel-van-der-kolk-how-trauma-lodges-in- the-body-revisited/

- Pollack, R. (2022). *Trust your intuition.* Muse Literary.

- Le Cunff, A.-L. (n.d.). The uncertain mind: How the brain handles the unknown. *Ness Labs.* https://nesslabs.com/uncertain-mind

- Linehan, M. (1993). *Cognitive behavioral treatment of borderline personality disorder.* Guilford Press.

- No author. (2021, June 16). Mindfulness for your health: The benefits of living moment to moment. *NIH News in Health.* https://newsinhealth.nih.gov/2021/06/mindfulness-your-health

- Cherry, K. (2022, September 2). Benefits of mindfulness. *Very Well Mind.* https://www.verywellmind.com/the-benefits-of-mindfulness- 5205137

- Katie, B. (2003). *Loving what is.* Three Rivers Press.

- Frankel, V. E. (2006). *Man's search for meaning.* Beacon Press.

- Salzberg, S. (2013, Spring). Mindfulness and difficult emotions. *Tricycle Magazine.* https://tricycle.org/magazine/mindfulness-and- difficult-emotions/

- Health Match Staff. (2022, May 18). Adrenaline anxiety: What is it and how can you manage it? *Health Match.* https://healthmatch.io/anxiety/how-to-reduce-adrenaline-anxiety

- McPhilips, K. (2020, April 8). The 5-4-3-2-1 grounding technique a mental health counselor swears by when thoughts spiral out of control. *Well+Good.* https://www.wellandgood.com/54321-grounding-technique/

- Gonzalez, G. (2014, February 13). Somatic experiencing – Orientation. *Eight Elements West.* https://www.eightelementswest.com/somatic-experiencing-orientation/

- Dana, D. (2018). *The polyvagal theory in therapy.* W.W. Norton & Company.

- Emmons, R. (2020). *The gratitude project: How the science of thankfulness can rewire our brains for resilience, optimism, and the greater good.* New Harbinger Publications.

- Kho, N. D. (2019). *The thank-you project: Cultivating gratitude one thank-you letter at a time.* Running Press Adult.

- Robinson, B.E. (2020, November 6). Why you hate uncertainty and how to cope. *Psychology Today.* https://www.psychologytoday.com/us/blog/the- right-mindset/202011/why-you-hate-uncertainty-and-how-cope

- Robson, D. (2021, October 26). Why we're so terrified of the unknown. *BBC.* https://www.bbc.com/worklife/article/20211022-why- were-so-terrified-of-the-unknown

- We Can Do Hard Things Podcast (Episode 130).

- Rodsky, E. (2019). *Fair play: A game-changing solution for when you have too much to do (and more life to live).* G.P. Putnam's Sons.

- Brown, B. (2010). *The gifts of imperfection: Let go of who you think you're supposed to be and embrace who you are.* Hazelden.

- Raypole, C. (2020, September 1). Positive affirmations – Too good to be true? *Healthline.* https://www.healthline.com/health/mental-health/do- affirmations-work

- Scult, M. (2023, April 24). Why positive affirmations can do more harm than good.

Psychology Today.
https://www.psychologytoday.com/ca/blog/the-big- reframe/202304/when-positive-affirmations-do-more-harm-than-good

- Neff, K. (n.d.). *Self-compassion.* https://www.self-compassion.org/

- Neff, K. (2011). *Self-compassion: The proven power of being kind to yourself.* William Morrow.

- Hayes, S. C., Smith, C., & Smith, S. (2005). *Get out of your mind and into your life: The new acceptance and commitment therapy.* New Harbinger Publications.

- Hebb, D. (1949). *The organization of behavior.* Psychology Press

About The Author

Noelle McWard Aquino is a psychotherapist in private practice in Chicago, IL. She developed the Anxiety Unpacked model to support her work with her anxious clients. Noelle speaks to both mental health professionals and non-clinical audiences about anxiety.

www.noellemcwardaquino.com or
noelle@noellemcwardaquino.com